CW00348301

IPSWICH T

AN A–Z

Dean Hayes

S.B. Publications

First published in 1998 by S. B. Publications,
c/o 19 Grove Road, Seaford, East Sussex BN25 1TP

©1998 Dean Hayes

ISBN 1 85770 174 7

Designed and typeset by CGB, Lewes
Printed by MFP Design and Print
Longford Trading Estate, Thomas Street,
Stretford, Manchester M32 0JT

DEDICATION

To Ipswich Town fans everywhere.

ACKNOWLEDGEMENTS

I SHOULD like to express my thanks to the following organisations for their help: Ipswich Town Football Club, The Association of Football Statisticians, The Football League, Ipswich Central Reference Library, The British Newspaper Library, The Harris Library, Preston.

Thanks also to the following individuals: Ben Hayes, Iain Price, Robert Lomas, and Stephen Whittle.

PICTURE CREDITS

ILLUSTRATIONS were kindly supplied by the *Lancashire Evening Post* and from the author's personal collection. The back cover photograph of the 1978 FA Cup winning team is by Owen Hines.

Front cover: Clockwise from top: Chris Kiwomya, Mick Mills, George Burley and Terry Butcher.

A

ABANDONED MATCHES

A MATCH which is called off by the referee while it is in progress because conditions do not permit it to be completed. Generally speaking, far fewer matches are now abandoned because if there is some doubt about the ability to play the full game, the match is more likely to be postponed.

The club's first Football League game to be abandoned was at Southend United on 24 December 1938. The game was called off at forty minutes because of a blizzard with the score 0–0. On 27 November 1948, Ipswich totally dominated their first round FA Cup tie against Aldershot and led 1–0 when, after sixty three minutes, the game had to be abandoned because of fog. The teams tried again a week later with Aldershot running out winners 3–0.

During the 1960–61 season, the game at Derby took three attempts to play. It was originally scheduled for 31 December 1960 but was postponed because the Baseball Ground was waterlogged. Just thirty eight minutes of the re-arranged match had been played on 28 January 1961 when referee Arthur Ellis had to call a halt to proceedings with County leading 2–1 as a downpour was making conditions just as bad as they had been for the first game. When they played the game at the end of the season, Ipswich won 4–1.

When Ipswich entertained Coventry City on 25 November 1972, a fuse blew in the local electricity substation and the floodlights went out with the Highfield Road club leading 1–0. When the game was replayed, goals from Whymark and Johnson gave Ipswich a 2–0 win. The last game involving Ipswich to be abandoned was on 11 December 1976 when the match against Newcastle United at St James' Park was called off at half-time because of icy conditions with the home side leading 1–0.

ACRES, BASIL

Full-back Basil Acres joined Ipswich as an amateur in the summer of 1951 and made his first team debut in a disastrous 5–1 defeat at Brighton and Hove Albion on 12 September 1951, a team that Town had beaten 5–0 at home a week earlier.

Acres developed into a strong-tackling defender with good distributional skills and in 1953–54 when the club won the Third Division (South) Championship, he was one of five players to appear in all fifty three League and Cup games. His only goal during that campaign in which he was part of a solid Town defence consisting of Feeney, Myles, Rees and Parker, was the winner on the ground he made his debut as Brighton were beaten 2–1.

When the club won the Third Division (South) Championship again in 1956–57, Acres lost his place to Larry Carberry halfway through the season and when he did return, he showed his versatility by playing in a variety of positions. In fact, in the last game of the season which Town had to win to overtake Torquay United and hope the Devon club did not win their game at Crystal Palace, Acres played at centre-forward and scored one of the goals in a 2–0 win at Southampton.

He went on to score six goals in 232 League and Cup games but at the end of the 1960–61 season he was forced to quit the game as a result of a troublesome ankle injury.

AGGREGATE SCORE

Ipswich's highest aggregate score in any competition came in the European Cup in September 1962 against Floriana of Malta, when they notched up fourteen goals over two legs. Ipswich won the first leg in Malta 4–1 and then 10–0 at Portman Road with Ray Crawford scoring five of the goals.

AMATEUR CUP

Ipswich entered the FA Amateur Cup in 1893–94, its inaugural season but after gaining a bye in the first qualifying round, lost 1–0 to Ilford. The following season, the club reached the last sixteen of the competition, only to lose 7–3 against Old Etonians after a replay. Over the next few years, the club had little success in the competition and met with some heavy defeats, none more so than a 10–0 reversal at Old Malvernians in 1901–02.

One of the club's best runs was in 1921–22 when they reached the Second Round proper before losing 5–0 at Barking. Town won five games to reach that stage including beating Lowestoft 7–0 with Frank Johnson scoring five of the goals. Town equalled this performance in 1935–36, the last time they entered the competition, but after wins over RAF Martlesham, Orwell Works (who were beaten 10–1), Walton United, Lowestoft Town and King's Lynn, they lost 4–2 at Kingstonians.

ANGLO-ITALIAN CUP

Ipswich first entered the much maligned competition in 1995–96 when their results against their Italian counterparts saw them beat Reggiana (home 2–1) and draw against Brescia (away 2–2) before winning the other two games against Foggia (away 1–0) and Salernitana (home 2–0).

The Portman Road club went out of the competition at the next stage when they lost 4–2 at home to Port Vale.

APPEARANCES

The players with the highest number of appearances for Ipswich Town FC are as follows:

	League	FA Cup	FLg Cup	Others	Total
Mick Mills	588(3)	57	43(1)	49	737(4)
John Wark	533(6)	55(3)	42(2)	39	670(11)
Paul Cooper	447	45	43	37	572
Mick Stockwell	420(21)	26(3)	36(4)	22(2)	504(30)
George Burley	394	43	35	28	500
Tommy Parker	428	37	0	0	465
Bill Baxter	409	23	22	5	459
John Elsworthy	396	27	6	4	433
Jason Dozzell	320(20)	22	31(1)	22	395(21)
Doug Rees	356	29	0	0	385

ATTENDANCE – AVERAGE

Ipswich Town's average home league attendances over the last ten years have been as follows:

1988–89	12,650	1993–94	16,382
1989–90	12,913	1994–95	16,818
1990–91	11,722	1995–96	12,604
1991–92	14,274	1996–97	11,953
1992–93	18,223	1997–98	14,973

ATTENDANCE – HIGHEST

The record attendance at Portman Road is 38,010 for the sixth round FA Cup game with Leeds United on 8 March 1975. The match ended 0–0 but Town went on to win the third replay at Filbert Street 3–2 with goals from Hamilton, Whymark and Woods.

ATTENDANCE – LOWEST

The lowest attendance at Portman Road is 3,116 for the visit of Leyton Orient in a Third Division (South) game on 25 March 1953. The visitors, who ended the season two places above Ipswich, won 1–0.

ATKINSON, DALIAN

A physically strong striker, Dalian Atkinson began his career with Ipswich Town, signing as an associated schoolboy in 1982 before becoming an apprentice two years later. He made his league debut as a substitute for the Blues away to Newcastle United on 15 March 1986 and impressed. After only occasional appearances for the club, he finally established a first team place in February 1988, scoring eight goals in just thirteen full appearances to the the end of the season. Included in this haul was a magnificent hat-trick in a 4–0 win over promotion bound Middlesbrough.

After a tour of Brazil with the England Under-20 squad, he was hoping for a place with the Under-21 side but unfortunately missed out on a chance to play against Sweden through injury. He had scored twenty one goals in sixty six League and Cup games when in the summer of 1989 he was transferred to Sheffield Wednesday for £450,000.

He immediately became a big favourite with the Hillsborough faithful but only stayed for twelve months before being sold to Spanish side, Real Sociedad. After one year in Spain where he scored twelve goals in twenty nine League games, he returned to England and Aston Villa.

A succession of niggling injuries prevented him from playing in more games than he did for Villa but many of his thirty four goals in his 106 first team outings were memorable efforts, perhaps none more so than his *Match of the Day* Goal of the Season competition winner against Wimbledon in 1992–93. After leaving Villa for Fenerbahce, he returned to English football with Manchester City.

AWAY MATCHES

Ipswich's best away win in the Football League came on 25 September 1982 when they won 6–0 at Notts County. The club have also won away 6–1 on two occasions – at Bristol Rovers on the opening day of the 1948–49 season and at Millwall in the sixth round of the 1977–78 FA Cup.

The club's worst defeat away from home is the 10–1 thrashing handed out by Fulham on Boxing Day 1963. The club have also conceded nine goals on three occasions – Notts County 2–9 (1948–49) Stoke City 1–9 (1963–64) and Manchester United 0–9 (1994–95).

AWAY SEASONS

The club's highest number of away wins came in 1953–54 when they won twelve of their twenty three matches in winning the Third Division (South) Championship.

In 1963–64, when the club finished bottom of the First Division, they failed to win one single away game.

B

BAILEY, ROY

GOALKEEPER Roy Bailey first made a name for himself when playing for Crystal Palace Reserves, saving three penalties in a match.

After returning from military service he established himself as Palace's first choice keeper and made 119 League and Cup appearances before Alf Ramsey signed him in March 1956. Arriving at Portman Road thirty six hours before the deadline, Bailey went straight into the side for the East Anglian derby at Carrow Road, only to be on the losing side as the Canaries won 3–2.

The following season, Bailey was the only ever-present as the club swept to the Third Division Championship, his displays being rated as on a par with Mick Burns, Town's custodian either side of the Second World War. After missing just four games in 1957–58 he was ever-present again for the next two seasons, appearing in eighty eight consecutive league games. In the 1959–60 season, he gained something of a reputation for saving penalties, doing so in four league games.

The Epsom-born 'keeper was one of five Ipswich players to win Championship medals for all three divisions with the club.

After playing in 346 League and Cup games for the Blues during his nine seasons with the club, he was given a free transfer and went to coach in South Africa. His son Gary Bailey kept goal for Manchester United and won full England honours.

BAIRD, HARRY

Belfast-born wing-half Harry Baird began his career with Linfield before signing for Manchester United in January 1937. He made his debut for the Old Trafford club in a 1–0 defeat at Sheffield Wednesday towards the end of that month but after appearing in fifty three first team games, he joined Huddersfield Town. His career with the Yorkshire club was interrupted by the war and although he won a full international cap for Northern Ireland, he only appeared in nineteen league games.

10

When the hostilities were over, he signed for Ipswich Town and made his debut in a 2–2 draw at Leyton Orient on the opening day of the 1946–47 season. An ever-present during 1947–48 when Town finished fourth in the Third Division (South) he went on to score seven goals in 227 League and Cup games before becoming the club's 'A' team coach at the end of the 1950–51 season, although he did appear in fourteen games the following season.

BAKER, GERRY

Gerry, the brother of England international centre-forward Joe Baker, began his career with Larkhall Thistle in Scotland before joining Chelsea. Unable to win a first team place at Stamford Bridge, he returned north of the border to sign for St Mirren. At Love Street he wrote himself into the record books when he scored ten of the club's goals in a 15–0 Scottish Cup win over Glasgow University. His prolific goalscoring for the Scottish club led to him joining Manchester City but after netting fourteen goals in thirty seven games he returned to Scotland to play for Hibernian.

Although he was brought up in Scotland, he had been born in New York and played international football for the United States. He left Easter Road in December 1963 to join Ipswich Town for a fee of £17,000 and so became the club's most expensive signing.

After making his debut in a goal-less draw at home to Blackburn Rovers, he scored in each of his next five appearances before netting hat-tricks against Tottenham Hotspur (away 3–6), Blackpool (home 4–3) and in the FA Cup tie against Oldham Athletic (home 6–3). His three goals at White Hart Lane is the only occasion an Ipswich player has scored a hat-trick and been on the losing side. He ended the season as the club's top scorer with eighteen goals in twenty two appearances.

Baker was the club's top scorer in season's 1964–65 (sixteen goals in thirty seven games) and 1965–66 (fifteen in forty three games) before becoming unsettled and going on the transfer list.

He continued to find the net on a regular basis but in November 1967, after scoring sixty six goals in 151 games, he left to join First Division Coventry City. Injuries hampered his career at Highfield Road and although he tried valiantly to continue playing, he finally had to admit defeat and quit league football.

BAXTER, BILL

Long-serving club captain Bill Baxter joined Ipswich Town in the summer of 1960 from Scottish junior club Broxburn Athletic. Signed with the intention of being cover for the club's first team regulars, he found himself pressed into service after an injury to Reg Pickett and made his debut in a 4–1 home win over Norwich City on 27 December 1960. He then played in the remaining nineteen games of the season as Town went on to win the Second Division championship.

In 1961–62 the strong-tackling wing-half missed just two games as the club swept to the League Championship. Having started his National Service on his arrival as Portman Road, his form that campaign led to him representing the Army team on several occasions and in the close season he toured the Far East with them.

He was ever-present in 1962–63 and he scored his first league goal for the club in a 1–1 draw at Fulham. Although Town finished bottom of the First Division in 1963–64, Baxter was the club's only ever-present, an achievement he repeated in season's 1965–66 and 1966–67. In 1967–68 he missed just one game as Town won the Second Division championship, appearing in 131 consecutive league games during this period of his Portman Road career.

Baxter went on to appear in 459 games for the club before leaving in sad circumstances. Following Town's exit from the League Cup at the hands of West Bromwich Albion, an article attributed to him appeared in a Sunday newspaper, berating the club. Unable to give a satisfactory explanation of this to manager Bobby Robson, he was suspended and relieved of the captaincy.

In March 1971 he left the club to join fellow Second Division promotion challengers, Hull City and went on to appear in twenty league games for the Boothferry Park club before following a loan spell with Watford, he ended his league career with Northampton Town.

BEATTIE, KEVIN

A product of the Ipswich Town youth policy masterminded by Bobby Robson, Carlisle-born Kevin Beattie made his league debut for the club on the opening day of the 1972–73 season in a 2–1 victory over Manchester United at Old Trafford. Two weeks later, Ipswich travelled to Leeds United where Beattie scored his first league goal in an exciting 3–3 draw.

The Portman Road club ended the 1972–73 season in fourth place, their best showing since they won the League Championship eleven years earlier. Beattie had played thirty eight league games in the heart of the Ipswich defence and had scored five goals. He was by now one of the game's greatest creative forces and was a huge favourite with the Ipswich crowd.

In the early part of the following season, Beattie in turned in some outstanding performances in an Ipswich side that hovered in mid-table before ending the season in fourth place. Along with captain Mick Mills he was one of the only two players who had started in all forty two league games for the club.

His fellow professionals were so impressed with his play that they selected him as the first PFA Young Player of the Year, an award presented to him by Leeds United manager, Don Revie.

The following season, the Leeds boss was appointed manager of England in succession to Joe Mercer. In his fourth match in charge, Revie selected Beattie in the centre of England's defence for their European Championship qualifier against Cyprus at Wembley. It was a game England won 5–0 with

Kevin Beattie

Malcolm MacDonald creating a post-war record by scoring all England's goals. The Ipswich player almost got his name on the scoresheet but in the process of scoring, he was adjudged to have fouled the goalkeeper. He went on to win nine caps for his country, all but one of them under Revie's management.

In 1978 Beattie was a member of the Ipswich team which beat Arsenal in the FA Cup Final. He was a player who could have become one of the all-time greats but he had to undergo five operations on his right knee in four years and after scoring thirty two goals for Ipswich in 307 first team games, he played briefly for Colchester United and Middlesbrough before the injury brought his playing career to a premature end in 1982.

BELL, DAVID

Scottish-born wing-half David Bell began his league career with Newcastle United but was unlucky with injuries at St James' Park and joined Derby County for £700. He took advantage of injuries to Ted Udall at Derby and established himself at right-back in County's First Division side of 1937–38. He left the Baseball Ground in October 1938 to join Ipswich Town in their first season in the Football League.

After winning their first two games in the Third Division (South) Town went nine games without a win before Bell made his debut in a 1–0 home win over Torquay United. There followed an upturn in the club's fortunes and they finished seventh at the end of the season. Sadly, Bell's career was then interrupted by the Second World War but when league football resumed in 1946–47, he played in forty league games as Town moved up to sixth place. He went on to play in 183 League and Cup games for the Portman Road club before retiring at the end of the 1949–50 season.

BEST, DAVID

GOALKEEPER David Best began his career with his then local club, Bournemouth, and made 230 league appearances for them before joining Oldham Athletic in September 1966. He had played in two league games short of a hundred for the Lancashire club when in October 1968 he signed for Ipswich Town.

The Wrexham-born Best made his debut for the Blues in a 2–1 win against Nottingham Forest in a game played at Notts County's Meadow Lane ground. He soon established himself as the club's first choice 'keeper and in 1969–70 kept eleven clean sheets in forty games as the club struggled to avoid relegation from the First Division.

The following season, Best was in goal when Ipswich visited Stamford Bridge to play Chelsea and conceded 'the goal that never was' in a 2–1 win for the home side. Later in that 1970–71 season, Best lost his place to Laurie Sivell and asked for a transfer because he wanted to play first team football. Surprisingly, no realistic offers were received and Best stayed at

Portman Road until 1974 when after making 199 League and Cup appearances he left to join Portsmouth. He made fifty six appearances for the Fratton Park club before returning to end his Football League career with his first club, Bournemouth.

BEST STARTS

Ipswich Town were unbeaten for the first fourteen games of the 1980–81 season when they won eight and drew six matches belore losing 1–0 at Brighton and Hove Albion on 11 November 1980. The club went on to finish the season as runners-up to First Division champions, Aston Villa.

BIGGEST DEFEATS

The club's biggest defeat in the Football League occurred on Boxing Day 1963 when the Blues were beaten 10–1 by Fulham at Craven Cottage. They also conceded ten goals on four occasions – Old Malvernians (1901–02 away 0–10); Eastbourne (1909–10 away 4–10); Ealing (1926–27 away 5–10); and Harwich and Parkeston (1927–28 away 1–10).

BIGGEST VICTORIES

The club's biggest victory in the Football League is 7–0, a scoreline achieved in three games – Portsmouth in 1964–65, Southampton in 1973–74, and West Bromwich Albion in 1976–77. On 25 September 1962, Ipswich beat Maltese side Floriana 10–0 in a European Cup preliminary round match.

During their pre-Football League days, the club scored eleven goals in a match on two occasions – Languard Fort (11–1 in the Suffolk Senior Cup match played at Bury St Edmunds in 1895–96) and Cromer (11–0 in the third qualifying round of the 1936–37 FA Cup competition). However, on 30 October 1880, East Samford were beaten 15–0 in a friendly, the biggest victory in the club's history.

BRAZIL, ALAN

Although the famous Celtic Boys Club was not officially linked with the Glasgow giants, the Parkhead side were usually quick to spot any available

Brazil adds another to his total of goals.

talent, but they overlooked Alan Brazil who joined Ipswich Town.
A Scottish Youth international, he made his league debut in a 2–1 defeat
at Manchester United in January 1978. He was a member of the entertain-
ing and highly successful side, built by Bobby Robson that challenged for
major honours and won the UEFA Cup in 1981. Having played for the
Scotland Under-21 team, Brazil made his full international debut against
Poland in May 1980 and during his stay at Portman Road, won eight
Under-21 and eleven full caps.

A consistent goalscorer, his best season was 1981–82 when he scored
twenty eight goals in forty four League and Cup games. On 16 February
1982, Southampton visited Portman Road as the league leaders and had
suffered only one defeat in their last thirteen matches. Brazil scored a hat-
trick within the space of five minutes in the first half and went on to net all
five goals in Town's 5–2 win.

He had scored eighty goals in 210 first team games when in March 1983
he joined Tottenham Hotspur for a fee of £450,000. Finding that his style
of play did not really fit in with that of Spurs, he was allowed to move on
for £750,000 to Manchester United, who had been keen to sign him before

he left East Anglia. Again Brazil was unable to recapture his outstanding form at Portman Road or adapt his play to the pattern of his club and after an unhappy time at Old Trafford, he joined Coventry City. At Highfield Road he began to rediscover his old touch but after five months returned to London, this time signing for Queen's Park Rangers. However, he played in only four league games for the Loftus Road club before suffering a serious back injury that forced him to retire from league football, although he continued to play in non-league circles.

BRENNAN, MARK

A skilful midfielder with a lovely left foot and good vision, the Lancashire-born Brennan made his league debut for Ipswich in a 1–0 home win over Arsenal in November 1983.

By the end of the season he had won a regular spot in the club's midfield and became a fixture at Portman Road over the next four years. He went on to score twenty four goals in 202 League and Cup games for the club before being transferred to Middlesbrough in the 1988 close season.

He settled well on Teeside but after two seasons in which the club struggled in the lower reaches, he moved on to Manchester City.

He found it difficult to win a regular place in City's midfield and in November 1992 he joined Oldham Athletic for a fee of £200,000. He was never a prolific goalscorer but he did achieve one memorable goal in the Premiership match against Chelsea, which the Latics won 3–1. Kevin Hitchcock came to the edge of the penalty area to clear a poor back pass and only succeeded in hacking the ball as far as the halfway line. The ball dropped at Brennan's feet and he lifted a shot over the goalkeeper from fully 60 yards for Oldham's third goal.

Having played in 415 League and Cup games for his four clubs, he was given a free transfer by Oldham at the end of the 1995–96 season.

BROGAN, FRANK

Beginning his career with Celtic, left-winger Frank Brogan was rated one of the best in Scotland when he joined the Blues in the summer of 1964.

 He had been selected as a reserve for the full Scotland team but was unable to win a regular place in the Parkhead Club's first team because of the form of John Hughes.

Brogan made his Ipswich debut in a goal-less draw at Cardiff City on the opening day of the 1965–66 seaon and by the end of the campaign had played in forty three League and Cup games – more than anyone else. He also netted his first hat-trick for the club in a 7–0 win over Portsmouth on 7 November 1964.

His second hat-trick for the Blues came two years later in a 6–1 defeat of Northampton Town. Two of his goals were from the penalty spot and this was the first occasion on which the club had scored from two penalties in a Football League match.

When Ipswich won the Second Division championship in 1967–68, Brogan was the Blue's leading scorer in the league with seventeen goals in thirty six games, including his third hat-trick for the club in a 5–0 win over Bristol City.

He continued to be an important member of the side in the top flight but

18

his goal output diminished. After playing the last of his 223 League and Cup games in which he scored sixty nine goals for the Blues at Everton, he left Portman Road to join Halifax Town, where he ended his league career.

BROTHERS

Despite the vast geographical disparity of their birthplaces, brothers David and Neil Gregory have both played for Ipswich Town. Midfield player David Gregory was born in Sudbury and made his debut against Chelsea on 22 December 1988, nearly two years after signing professional forms. He went on to appear in thirty four league games for the club, half of which were as a substitute before joining Peterbrough United on a free transfer in July 1995.

Hard-running striker Neil Gregory was born in Ndola, Zambia and became a full-time professional during the 1992 close season. He made his debut against Wimbledon on 16 December 1994 but in January 1998 after scoring nine goals in fifty one League and Cup games including a hat-trick in a 3–1 win over Sheffield United, he joined Colchester United.

When they played alongside each other for Colchester United at Wembley, they became the first brothers to appear in a play-off final.

BUCKETS OF SALT

On 2 January 1965, Ipswich entertained Norwich City at Portman Road in a Second Division match. City's Tommy Bryceland had to leave the field midway through the first half, leaving the Canaries with ten men. Ipswich scored twice at Churchman's End in the first half and on both occasions, Kevin Keelan in the Norwich goal lost his footing.

At half-time the temperature had dropped below freezing and so the referee asked the groundstaff to spread salt in the goalmouth in the interest of safety. Not surprisingly the Norwich supporters thought that the groundstaff were making things easier for the home side's defenders and scuffles broke out during which much of the salt was spilt. Whether the little that was spread made much difference is hard to determine as Town ran out winners 3–0.

George Burley, Ipswich's 1976/77 Player of the Year.

BURLEY, GEORGE

An adventurous defender, George Burley joined Ipswich Town straight from school and made a memorable debut at the age of seventeen years 209 days when he completely marked George Best out of the game in a 2–0 defeat against Manchester United at Old Trafford on 29 December 1973.

Over the next twelve seasons, Burley missed very few games and in 1975–76 when the club finished sixth in Division One, he was ever-present. In 1976–77 he was voted the club's Player of the Year and in 1978 won an FA Cup winners' medal as a Roger Osborne goal was enough to beat Arsenal in the Wembley final. Burley, who had won international honours for Scotland at Schoolboy and Under-21 level won the first of eleven full caps for his country in 1979 when he played against Wales.

Sadly, he was not in the Ipswich side that beat AZ67 Alkmaar to win the UEFA Cup in 1980–81 having severely damaged his knee ligaments in an FA Cup tie at Shrewsbury Town.

Burley went on to appear in exactly 500 first team games for Ipswich before leaving Portman Road in September 1985 to join Sunderland. He played in fifty four league games for the Wearsiders before ending his career with Gillingham.

After spells as manager of Ayr United and coach of Motherwell, he took charge at Colchester United but in December 1994 his career completed full circle when he returned to Ipswich as manager. At the time of his appointment, the club were firmly rooted to the foot of the Premier League and though they beat Leicester City 4–1 and then won their first victory at Anfield, the Blues were relegated. After leading the club to seventh in Division One in 1995–96, Burley took the Blues to the play-offs for the next two seasons where they failed to reach their target of a return to the Premier League.

BURNS, MICK

Goalkeeper Mick Burns began his Football League career with Preston North End and appeared for the Deepdale club in their 3–1 FA Cup Final defeat by Sunderland at Wembley in 1937. He joined Ipswich Town in the summer of 1938 and went straight into the club's first team, making his debut in a 4–2 home win over Southend United. He went on to be one of only two ever-presents in that 1938–39 season, keeping sixteen clean sheets as the club finished seventh in the Third Division (South).

After starring in the 2–1 Jubilee Fund match victory over Norwich City, Burns guested for the Canaries during the war years before returning to Portman Road for the start of the 1946–47 season. He missed just one game that season as Town finished sixth in the Third Division (South) but midway through the following season he lost his place to Tom Brown and did not play another first team game until 1950–51 when he returned as the club's first choice 'keeper. He played the last of his 176 games for Ipswich in an FA Cup tie against Gateshead on 12 January 1952 at the age of forty three years 219 days. For the record, the game ended all square at 2–2 with Neil Myles scoring a last minute penalty for Town.

BUTCHER, TERRY

Terry Butcher, pictured left, was born in Singapore where his father was in the Royal Navy. A competitive and commanding central defender, he made his Ipswich Town debut in a 1–0 defeat at Everton in April 1978 before establishing himself as a first team regular the following season.

In 1980, Butcher won his first full cap for England when he played against Australia after winning honours at Under-21 and B international level. Later that season, he helped Ipswich to a UEFA Cup Final victory over AZ67 Alkmaar and to runners-up in the First Division. He continued to be a mainstay of the Ipswich defence and in 1982–83 was an ever-present, also the first campaign since his debut season that he failed to find the net. When Mick Mills left Portman Road to join Southampton Butcher, who was

Player of the Year in 1984–85, became captain. In the summer of 1986, after the club had been relegated, he left after making 344 first team appearances. He joined Glasgow Rangers for a fee of £725,000 and at Ibrox Park he won three Scottish Premier League championship medals, three Scottish League Cup winners' medals and a Scottish Cup runners-up medal.

Butcher who won seventy seven caps for his country, played in three World Cup finals including skippering them to the semi-finals against West Germany in 1990.

He fell out with Rangers' manager Graeme Souness, and in November 1990 joined Coventry City as player/manager. In his first season at Highfield Road, the Sky Blues struggled against relegation but eventually pulled clear to safety. Forced to sack his one-time Ipswich Town colleague Mick Mills, he too lost his job when he refused to negotiate a new 'manager only' contract after the club chairman felt he should take a cut in salary as he was suffering from a long-term injury.

Following the sacking of Malcolm Crosby, Butcher became player/manager of Sunderland in February 1993 but was dismissed when the club ended the season in twenty first place in the Barclays League Division One.

He now runs the Old Manor Hotel in Bridge of Allen near Stirling but still has many connections with the game including his weekly column in the *Scottish Daily Express* and his regular commentaries on Sky Television.

C

CAPACITY

THE total capacity of Portman Road in 1998–99 was 22,600.

CAPS

The most capped player in the club's history is Allan Hunter who won forty seven caps for Northern Ireland.

CAPS (ENGLAND)

The first Ipswich player to be capped by England was Ray Crawford when he played against Northern Ireland in 1962. The most capped player is Terry Butcher with forty five caps.

CAPS (NORTHERN IRELAND)

The first Ipswich players to be capped by Northern Ireland were Bryan Hamilton and Allan Hunter when they played against USSR in 1972. The most capped player is Allan Hunter with forty seven caps.

CAPS (SCOTLAND)

The first Ipswich players to be capped by Scotland were George Burley and John Wark when they played against Wales in 1979. The most capped player is John Wark with twenty six caps.

CAPS (WALES)

The first Ipswich player to be capped by Wales was William Reed when he played against Scotland in 1955. The most capped players are Mick Hill, Cyril Lea and William Reed with two caps each.

CAPTAINS

Jimmy McLuckie who captained Ipswich Town to the Southern League Championship in 1936–37 was also skipper when the club played its first season of league football in 1938–39. He made 124 league appearances before leaving to manage Clacton Town.

Tommy Parker played in 475 first team games, scoring ninety five goals and captained the club from 1951 to 1956. During that time, the Blues won the Third Division (South) championship in 1953–54. In 1956–57 Doug Rees skippered the club to another Third Division (South) title after their relegation in 1954–55.

When Ipswich won the Second Division and League Championship titles in successive seasons, 1960–61 and 1961–62, they were captained by former West Ham United centre-half, Andy Nelson. One of the members of those successful Ipswich Town sides was Bill Baxter. He went on to play in 459 first team games and captained the side to the Second Division championship in 1967–68.

One of the most popular and successful of Ipswich town captains has been Mick Mills. The England international, who holds the club appearance record, skippered the Blues for twelve seasons and led them to success in the 1978 FA Cup Final and the UEFA Cup Final of 1980–81.

CARBERRY, LARRY

Bootle-born full-back Larry Carberry could have joined his local club, Liverpool, but after doing his National Service in the King's Regiment at Bury St Edmunds he was persuaded by Ipswich manager Alf Ramsey to join the Portman Road club.

He made his first team debut in a 4–0 home win over Queen's Park Rangers and went on to appear in twenty five games as the club won the Third Division (South) championship. The following season he represented the FA XI against the RAF at Meadow Lane and against the Army at Old Trafford. He was also selected as a travelling reserve for the England Under-23 side against Romania.

Over the next few seasons, Carberry established himself as one of the top defenders outside the top flight and in 1960–61 was ever-present as the club won the Second Division championship. The Ipswich defender played in all the games in 1961–62 as the club won the First Division Championship and was one of five players to win championship medals for all three divisions with the Portman Road club. At the start of the following season, Carberry hurt his ankle in the FA Charity Shield match against

Tottenham Hotspur at Portman Road and he was forced to miss a number of games through injury.

He went on to play in 285 games for the club before leaving at the end of the 1964–65 season to join Barrow. He appeared in just seventeen league games for the Holker Street club before hanging up his boots.

CARROLL, TOMMY

Dublin-born full-back Tommy Carroll began his career with Shelbourne where he won an Irish League Championship medal in 1962. He later starred in both the European Cup and European Cup Winners' Cup for the Irish club and in his time with them, appeared in every outfield position. After a spell playing non-league football for Cambridge City, he joined Ipswich Town in the summer of 1966 but had to wait until March 1967 before making his first team debut in a 1–1 draw at Hull City.

Capped seventeen times by the Republic of Ireland, Carroll was an important member of the club's 1967–68 Second Division championship-winning side, though he suffered with injuries during Town's first season back in the top flight. In 1969–70, Carroll was the club's only ever–present but after that he became unsettled and in October 1971, after appearing in 126 first team games, he left Portman Road to join Birmingham City.

A player who always believed in trying to play his way out of difficult situations, Carroll had appeared in just forty seven games for the St Andrew's club when he was forced to quit competitive football through injury.

CENTURIES

There are four instances of individual players who have scored 100 or more league goals for Ipswich Town. Ray Crawford is the greatest goalscorer with 204 strikes in his Ipswich career (1958–1969). Other centurions are Ted Phillips with 161 goals, John Wark with 135 and Tom Garneys with 123.

Mick Mills holds the club record for the most consective league appearances –198. Other players to have made more than 100 consecutive appearances during their careers are Steve McCall, 166; Jimmy Leadbetter, 138; Bill Baxter, 131; Ted Phillips, 128; John Wark, 127; George Rumbold 119; Neil Myles, 110; and Tom Brown, 109.

CHAMPIONSHIPS

Ipswich Town have won a divisional championship on six occasions. The first of these was in 1953–54 when after nine seasons of league football, the club won the Third Division (South) championship. They won their first four matches of the season and during one stage of the campaign, won eight consecutive matches. They were unbeaten in their last ten matches of the season and beat Brighton by three points to finish with the following record.

P	W	D	L	F	A	Pts
46	27	10	9	82	51	64

The club won the Third Division (South) championship for a second time in 1956–57 despite losing their first three games of the season. Ted Phillips scored forty one goals in forty one games to become the leading goalscorer in the entire Football League and included in his total were five hat-tricks. Town won six and drew one of their last seven matches to take the title on goal average from Torquay United.

P	W	D	L	F	A	Pts
46	25	9	12	101	54	59

In 1960–61, Ipswich won the Second Division championship in what was their Jubilee season. Midway through the campaign the club went 13 games without defeat including winning both matches against Norwich City and ended the season a point ahead of Sheffield United with the following record.

P	W	D	L	F	A	Pts
42	26	7	9	100	55	59

The following season of 1961–62 saw Ray Crawford and Ted Phillips score sixty one goals between them as Ipswich won the First Division championship. That they did so was down to manager, Alf Ramsey, who innovatively used his wingers in midfield. The club began the season badly, taking only one point from their first three matches but Ramsey stuck to his tactics and the results started coming.

P	W	D	L	F	A	Pts
42	24	8	10	93	67	56

Ipswich won the Second Division championship in 1967–68 after conceding just one goal in the opening five matches. Although they were always in the group of promotion contenders, they tended to draw too many matches. However, they were unbeaten for the last fifteen matches of the season and won the title with the following record.

P	W	D	L	F	A	Pts
42	22	15	5	79	44	59

Ipswich last won a divisional championship in 1991–92 when despite failing to win a match in eight consecutive games midway through the season, they won five games in succession to finish the season four points ahead of Middlesbrough with Chris Kiwomya the club's leading scorer.

P	W	D	L	F	A	Pts
46	24	12	10	70	50	84

CHAPLAINCY

Chaplaincy in football developed so that the chaplain became closely involved with the club, being known to players and non-playing staff. He tries to be concerned for all at the club and usually has a regular time to visit the ground – although the amount of time varies from club to club. Ipswich Town's chaplain is the Reverend Philip Miller.

CHARITY SHIELD

Ipswich Town have appeared in the FA Charity Shield on two occasions. The first on 11 August 1962 saw FA Cup winners' Tottenham Hotspur beat Ipswich 5–1 at Portman Road. Full-back Larry Carberry injured his ankle shortly before half-time but as the home side were already two goals down, it is unlikely that it influenced the final outcome. The club's second appearance in the Charity Shield was at Wembley on 12 August 1978 against league champions Nottingham Forest. Unfortunately, the club's defeat was even heavier than in their first appearance in the Charity Shield as Forest won 5–0.

CLEAN SHEET

This is the colloquial expression to describe a goalkeeper's performance when he does not concede a goal. Paul Cooper in 1979–80 had nineteen clean sheets from forty league appearances plus another eleven in cup competitions.

COLOURS

Ipswich Town first played in dark blue shirts with a white crest, although there were occasions in the club's early years when players appeared in all shades of blue. Indeed when they visited Norwich City during the 1903–04 season, the team turned out in an assortment of colours – chocolate, red, pink and different shades of blue.

In 1928–29 the club's colours changed to blue and white striped shirts, blue shorts and amber socks, but eight seasons later a new strip of blue shirts with white sleeves and white shorts was chosen as professional football arrived at Portman Road.

The club's next change of colours was in 1964–65 when they played in all blue, however many supporters still preferred the variety provided by the use of white. In 1977–78 the team had yet another new strip with white stripes down the arms of the blue shirt and blue stripes on the white shorts and a change strip of white shirts and black shorts. In 1981–82, the club wore their change strip of scarlet shirts, black shorts and scarlet socks for the first time. There was an adaptation to the playing strip three seasons later when a wide red band across the chest incorporating the sponsor's name was added.

The club's present colours are blue shirts, white shorts and blue stockings, and the change colours are orange shirts, navy shorts and orange stockings.

CONSECUTIVE HOME GAMES

Ipswich Town played an extraordinary intense sequence of six home games in succession in just twenty five days – from 27 January to 21 February 1981 – and won them all.

Date	Opponents	Competition	Score
27.01.1981	Shrewsbury Town	FA Cup	3–0
31.01.1981	Stoke City	Division One	4–0
07.02.1981	Crystal Palace	Division One	3–2
14.02.1981	Charlton Athletic	FA Cup	2–0
17.02.1981	Middlesbrough	Division One	1–0
21.02.1981	Wolverhampton Wands	Division One	3–1

Penalty saving expert, Paul Cooper, appeared for Ipswich in a total of 572 first team games.

CONSECUTIVE SCORING – LONGEST SEQUENCE

Tom Garney and Ted Phillips share the club record for consecutive scoring when they were on target in eight consecutive league games. Tom Garney's first goal came in a 4–2 home win over Bristol City on 2 November 1957 and ended with the winning goal in a 2–1 defeat of Blackburn Rovers, also at Portman Road on 21 December 1957.

Ted Phillips netted his first goal in a 1–1 draw at Bristol Rovers on 3 September 1960 and hit his last, his tenth goal, in a 2–0 win at Charlton Athletic on 8 October 1960. Phillips went on to score thirty goals as Town won the Second Division championship.

COOPER, PAUL

'Super Cooper' joined Ipswich Town from Birmingham City in 1974 for £27,000 – a fee which in retrospect was ridiculously small for the service and skill this goalkeeper gave to the Portman Road club. Initially signed on loan, his first match for the club was away against champions-to-be Leeds United, who won 3–2.

After winning a regular place in the Ipswich side at the beginning of the 1975–76 season, he was the club's first choice 'keeper for the next twelve seasons, appearing in a total of 572 first team games.

He learned to live with the slightly embarrassing situation of being the only uncapped player in the Ipswich Town side. The biggest consolation to him in this personal disappointment was that he was plying his trade in an era when there were two of the most outstanding England goalkeepers of any age in Peter Shilton and Ray Clemence. But he did not do so badly with other honours, collecting an FA Cup winners' medal when the Blues beat Arsenal and a UEFA Cup winners' medal when AZ67 Alkmaar were beaten in the two–legged final.

Cooper became something of an expert at saving penalties. He studied the technique of the leading penalty-takers and weighed up the chance of which way they would shoot and the intensity of the shot as well. This brought him phenomenal success and succeeded in creating grave doubts among the penalty 'kings' – a serious psychological disadvantage discovered by Liam Brady, Gerry Francis, Mickey Thomas and Terry McDermott amongst others when they tried to beat Cooper.

He left Portman Road in the summer of 1987 to play for Leicester City, later having a spell with Manchester City, for whom he scored an own goal before ending his League career with Stockport County.

CRANSON, IAN

Strong in the air and with sound distribution, central defender Ian Cranson worked his way through the club's ranks before making his first team debut for the Portman Road side in a 4–0 defeat at Aston Villa on 17 December 1983. Over the next five seasons, Cranson was capped five times by England at Under–21 level and made 165 first team appearances for Ipswich.

In March 1988 he joined Sheffield Wednesday but 16 months later he was on his way to Stoke City after just 34 League and Cup appearances for the Hillsborough club.

He became the Potters' record signing, costing the then Victoria Ground club 450,000. He had a problem knee which reduced his pace and at the end of the 1990–91 season he was offered reduced terms which technically entitled him to a free transfer but despite interest from Scottish Premier League sides, Hearts and Dunfermline Athletic, he stayed and went on to make 281 appearances for the club.

CRAWFORD, RAY

Ray Crawford began his league career with his home town club, Portsmouth, and made his debut for the Fratton Park club against Burnley on the opening day of the 1957–58 season.

After netting twelve goals in twenty two games for Pompey, he joined Ipswich in September 1958 and played his first game the following month, scoring both his side's goals in a 4–2 defeat at Swansea. That season he was the club's top scorer with twenty five goals in thirty league games including a hat-trick at Portman Road in the return game against Swansea Town and another in a 5–3 win over Brighton and Hove Albion.

Crawford and Ted Phillips soon developed a fine understanding and in 1959–60, the pair scored forty two league goals of which Crawford netted eighteen.

In 1960–61 when Town won the Second Division championship,

Crawford had a remarkable season, scoring forty of the club's 100 league goals. He scored three hat-tricks, two of which were away from home and only one at Portman Road – Brighton and Hove Albion (away 4–2), Leeds United (away 5–2) and Leyton Orient (home 6–2).

The following season, Crawford scored thirty three goals in forty one league games as Ipswich won the League Championship and scored the club's only hat-trick in a 5–2 home win over Chelsea. Also during that campaign, Crawford became the first Ipswich player to gain an England cap while on the club's books when he played against Ireland at Wembley. The Ipswich player provided the cross for Bobby Charlton to score in a 1–1 draw. Later that season he scored in England's 3–1 win over Austria and also played twice for the Football League against the Irish League in Belfast, when he scored twice in a 6–1 win and the Scottish League at Villa Park.

Crawford had another outstanding season in 1962–63, playing in every league match and scoring twenty five goals including all three goals in a 3–0 win over Sheffield Wednesday. It was also the club's first experience of European football and when they beat the Maltese champions Floriana 10–0 at home, Ray Crawford scored five of the goals to establish a scoring record for any British player in any European competition – since equalled by Chelsea's Peter Osgood. The 1962–63 campaign saw Crawford continue to represent the Football League and in the game against the Irish League at Carrow Road, he netted a hat-trick.

In September 1963, Crawford was surprisingly allowed to leave Portman Road and join Wolverhampton Wanderers but after scoring thirty nine goals in fifty seven league games for the Molineux club, he signed for West Bromwich Albion.

In March 1966, Ipswich manager Bill McGarry brought Crawford back to East Anglia, the Portsmouth-born centre-forward never having really settled with either of the Midlands clubs. He top-scored in 1966–67 with twenty one goals including another hat-trick in a 5–4 home win over Hull City and the following season scored four goals in a 5–2 League Cup victory over Southampton.

In March 1969, after scoring 228 goals in 354 games, Crawford left Ipswich to join Charlton Athletic before entering non-league football with Kettering Town. In 1970–71 he was brought back to the Football League by Colchester United and scored both their goals in a 3–2 defeat by First Division Leeds United in the fourth round of the FA Cup. In the first round he had scored a hat-trick in a 3–0 win over Ringmer to become the first player to score hat-tricks in the Football League, League Cup, FA Cup and European Cup.

CROWD TROUBLE

However unwelcome, crowd disturbances are far from a modern phenomenon at first class football matches. Behaviour at Portman Road has usually been of a high standard and although Town supporters are well renowned for voicing their opinions at suspect referees, the occasions when their demonstrations boil over are very rare indeed.

However, on 8 December 1900 King's Lynn visited Portman Road and won by the only goal of the game. After the match had finished, one of the visitors' players was hit by one of the crowd, who was later arrested.

On 15 April 1972, Ipswich entertained Sheffield United. The referee awarded the Blades a penalty and Jefferson and Harper were booked for protesting. Laurie Sivell made a fine diving save but despite this, Harper continued to make comments to the referee and was sent off. This resulted in cushions being thrown on to the pitch at the final whistle as the referee received a police escort.

The worst crowd trouble in a match involving Ipswich Town came in the sixth round FA Cup tie at Millwall on 11 March 1978. Although Ipswich won 6–1 with Paul Mariner scoring a hat-trick, the game was to be better remembered for the gangs of Millwall supporters who attacked the Ipswich fans and invaded the pitch in the half, causing the referee to take the players off the field for eighteen minutes while the police tried to restore order. Even after the match had finished, attacks on Ipswich supporters and their cars and coaches continued – it was a bad day for football but thankfully there were no serious injuries.

D

D'AVRAY, MICH

SOUTH African-born forward Mich D'Avray made his first team debut as a substitute for John Wark in a 3–1 home win over Southampton on 24 November 1979 before making his full debut a week later at Coventry City. The following season when Town finished runners-up to Aston Villa in the First Division, D'Avray scored his first goal for the club in a 3–1 defeat of Leicester City.

In April 1983, D'Avray at last received his British passport and went on to win two Under-21 caps for England as an over-age player, scoring on his debut in a 3–1 win over Italy in the semifinal first leg of the European Under-21 championships.

It was 1984–85 before he established himself as a first team regular at Portman Road and although he suffered from injuries and had a loan spell at Leicester City towards the end of his Ipswich career, he went on to score thrity seven goals in 211 league games for the Suffolk club.

DEBUTS

Colin Viljoen grabbed the headlines on his debut for Ipswich Town on 25 March 1967. He scored a hat-trick as Portsmouth were beaten 4–2 after the Fratton Park side had been two goals up inside the first quarter of an hour.

DEFEATS – FEWEST

During the 1967–68 season, Ipswich went through the forty two match programme and only suffered five defeats as they won the Second Division championship.

DEFEATS – MOST

Ipswich Town's total of twenty nine defeats during the 1994–95 season is the worst in the club's history. Not surprisingly, they finished bottom of the Premier League and were relegated.

DEFEATS – WORST

Ipswich's record defeat was when Fulham beat them 10–1 at Craven Cottage on 26 December 1963. At the end of that season, the club finished bottom of the First Division and were relegated.

On 4 March 1995, Ipswich were beaten 9–0 by Manchester United at Old Trafford with Andy Cole scoring five of the goals. The club also had nine goals put past them in the league on two other occasions – on 9 September 1948 when they lost 9–2 at Notts County and on 21 March 1964 when Stoke City beat them 9–0 at the Victoria Ground.

DEFENSIVE RECORDS

Ipswich's best defensive record was established in season's 1976–77 and 1979–80 when the club conceded just thirty nine goals and on both occasions ended the season in third place in the First Division.

The club's worst defensive record was in the 1963–64 relegation season when they let in 121 goals to finish bottom of the First Division.

DISMISSALS

Tom Haward became the first Ipswich player to be sent off during a game when the Portman Road club visited Framlingham College on 6 November

1897. He was later suspended for fourteen days for dangerous play.

One of the most unusual dismissals of an Ipswich player came in the FA Amateur Cup on 18 November 1933 when the Blues played Lowestoft Town in the Divisional Final. Town were 2–0 up when full-back Dick Manning went behind the goal to receive some treatment from Herbert Dainty, the club's trainer. The referee came over and asked Manning who had given him permission to leave the field. The Town defender failed to answer to the referee's satisfaction and the official told him to get off. Fortunately, Ipswich went on to win 3–1.

The only time an Ipswich goalkeeper has been dismissed in a competitive match came on 2 November 1935 when Henderson the Town 'keeper was sent off in the Eastern Counties League match at Yarmouth Town. Not surprisingly, the home side went on to win 2–0.

On 29 April 1950, Sam McCrory became the first Ipswich player to receive his marching orders in a Football League match when the Portman Road club were beaten 5–0 at Aldershot. Derek Jefferson was the first Ipswich player to be sent off at Portman Road and only the second ever in a Football League game when Chelsea won 3–1 on Boxing Day 1968.

DOZZELL, JASON

Jason Dozzell actually made his Football League debut while still an associated schools player, coming on as a substitute at home to Coventry City on 4 February 1984 and scoring in a 3–1 victory. At sixteen years and fifty six days old, he is the youngest player to have appeared in a league match for Ipswich Town. In 1985–86 he won a regular place in the side but it was not enough to save the Blues from relegation to the Second Division.

He was an ever–present in Town's team the following season and yet again in 1989–90. At the beginning of the 1990–91 season, he lost his place but when manager John Lyall restored him to the side, it was in a forward position rather than his usual midfield. He continued to play in this role during the club's Second Division championship winning season of 1991–92 when he partnered Chris Kiwomya. Dozzell scored eleven goals in forty five league games plus another four in five FA Cup games. In 1992–93 during the club's first season in the Premier League, he missed just one game but played in a variety of positions – midfield, striker and even central defence.

Despite being offered a long term contract, Dozzell, one of only nine players to play in more than 400 first team games, left Portman Road in the summer of 1993 to join Tottenham Hotspur for £1.9 million.

Often the scorer of crucial goals, his time at White Hart Lane was hampered by injuries and in five seasons at the club he only appeared in ninety nine League and Cup games before returning to Portman Road for a short spell before signing for Northampton Town.

DRAWS

Ipswich Town played their greatest number of drawn league matches in a single season in 1990–91 when eighteen of their matches ended all square, and their fewest in 1947–48 when only three of their matches were drawn. The club's highest scoring draw is 4–4, a scoreline in four home games – Leyton Orient in 1949–50; Crystal Palace in1949–50; Rotherham United in 1964–65; and Charlton Athletic in1990–91.

DUNCAN, JOHN

John Duncan was a Scotland schoolboys triallist who turned professional with his home club, Dundee, before being farmed out to Broughty Athletic. However, he was soon in the Dundee side, showing an eye for the goals that led to him being selected as non-playing substitute for the full Scotland side before appearing for the Scottish League against the Football League in 1973.

In 1974 he won a Scottish League Cup winners' medal when Dundee beat Celtic 1–0 in the final but in October of that year he joined Tottenham Hotspur for £150,000.

Lethal inside the penalty area, he ended his first season at White Hart

Lane as the club's top scorer. Although a back injury forced him to miss most of the 1976–77 season he went on to score seventy five goals in 145 games before leaving to play for Derby County in September 1978. Recurring back injury problems restricted Duncan to only thirty seven appearances for the Rams and he moved to Scunthorpe, quickly taking over as manager.

He was badly treated by Scunthorpe who sacked him to make way for Allan Clarke. He joined Hartlepool United but after only two months in charge, moved to Chesterfield and led them to the Fourth Division championship in 1985.

In the summer of 1987 he accepted an offer to manage Ipswich Town but after three seasons of the club finishing in mid-table, he was dismissed when they failed to make the 1990 promotion play offs.

After a spell in radio journalism and teaching, he was once again appointed manager of Chesterfield and in 1996–97 led them to the FA Cup semi-finals.

DUNCAN, SCOTT

Dumbarton–Born Adam Scott Duncan began his career with his home club before joining Newcastle United in March 1908. A fast, ball-playing winger, he was part of the Magpies' side that won the League Championship in 1908–09 and the FA Cup the following season. In 1911 he played for the Anglo-Scots in an international trial game but after scoring twelve goals in eighty one games, he left St James' Park to join Glasgow Rangers for a fee of £600. Later he again played for Dumbarton and then joined Cowdenbeath before hanging up his boots.

After managing Hamilton Academicals and Cowdenbeath, he took charge at Manchester United on a salary reported to be £800 per annum. In his first two seasons with the club he spent a great deal of money but failed to produce good results despite his financial outlay. In 1933–34 United just escaped relegation but two years later he led them to the Second Division championship.

Unfortunately, United were relegated after just one season in the top flight.

After Ipswich Town became a professional club in 1936, Chairman Captain J M Cobbold asked the secretary of the FA, Stanley Rous, to recommend a possible manager. Rous reported that Scott Duncan was considered the best. Cobbold drove to Manchester and invited Duncan to return with him to Ipswich.

Within a year, the club had been elected to the Football League and Duncan who was to stay at Portman Road for eighteen years, transformed the non-league side into one capable of reaching the Second Division when they won the Third Division (South) championship in 1953–54.

Sadly the club were relegated the following season and Duncan stepped down to be replaced by Alf Ramsey, although he stayed on at the club as secretary for a further three years.

E

EARLY GOALS

IPSWICH Town scored two goals within the first minute of the start of the Third Division (South) match against Brentford on 22 September 1956, before going on to win 4–0. Wilf Grant scored two of the goals whilst Tom Garneys and Doug Milward scored one goal apiece.

EARLY GROUNDS

The club's first ground was on Broom Hill, Norwich Road, where the players changed in a shed and then at the nearby Inkerman pub, which still exists today.

By 1883, the club had rented a better pitch on the lower slope of Broom Hill, called Brook's Hall. This is where the Orwell Works team played a where a floodlit game featuring the rugby club, Ipswich FC, had been staged in December 1878.

EAST ANGLIAN CUP

After winning their first match in the competition, 2–1 against Newmarket, Ipswich went out at home to Chelmsford by a similar scoreline in round two. In fact, over the five seasons that they took part in the competition, they never did very well and suffered some heavy defeats, notably in 1927–27 when they lost to Chelmsford 0–8; to Harwich and Parkeston 1–10 in 1927–28; and to Cambridge Town 0–6 in 1929–30.

EAST COAST FLOODS

One of the most dramatic events in the club's history occurred over the weekend of 31 January/1 February 1953 – the disastrous East Coast floods.

Arriving back from their match at Torquay United, which Town had lost 4–1, at 1pm. on the Sunday, the team was marooned at Ipwich Station for between four and five hours. A flood tide had caused the River Gipping to overflow and within a matter of minutes, Portman Road was under three feet of water. Although a pump was used to remove water from the main stand enclosure, a dyke was formed and fish caught there.

Just over three weeks later, a strong Ipswich Town team beat a Nore Command Royal Navy XI 3–1 in aid of the East Coast Flood Relief Fund, in a match which raised £158 2s 6d.

EASTERN COUNTIES LEAGUE

The club's first team competed in the Eastern Counties League for just one season, 1935–36. Their first match saw them lose 4–0 at Lowestoft Town, the club that went on to win the championship. Town finished in sixth place, with their best win being 10–2 against Thetford.

EIRE

The first Ipswich player to be capped by the Republic of Ireland was Tommy Carroll when he played against Poland in 1968. The most capped player is Kevin O'Callaghan with seventeen caps.

ELECTION TO THE LEAGUE

Ipswich Town made rapid progress towards Football League status in the 1930s. In 1934–35 they were still playing in the Southern Amateur League along with teams such as the Civil Service, Catford Wanderers and a variety of banks – among them Barclays, Lloyds, Midland, Westminster and even the Bank of England.

After finishing fourth that season they switched to the Eastern Counties League in 1935–36, finishing sixth and entered the Southern League in 1936–37 after turning professional. They won the championship at the first attempt and applied for election to the Third Division (South).

The result of the poll was Exeter City forty votes, Aldershot thirty four and Ipswich Town thirty four. Exeter and Aldershot were re-elected. Although Ipswich only finished third in the Southern League in 1937–38, they polled thirty six votes at the annual meeting of the Football League, compared with Walsall's thirty four and Gillingham's twenty eight, and were elected.

ELSWORTHY, JOHN

Wing-half John Elsworthy joined the club from Newport in the summer of 1949 and gave fifteen years loyal service to the Portman Road club, winning First, Second and two Third Division (South) championship medals.

He made his first team debut in a 4–0 home defeat by Notts County on 27 December 1949, but shortly afterwards went to do his National Service. When he was demobbed and was able to play football on a full-time basis, he turned in performances that led to a number of top clubs, notably Liverpool, expressing a strong interest in him. But ironically it was around this time that he began to lose form and his place in the Ipswich line-up.

On Boxing Day 1953 he scored his only hat-trick for the club in a 4–1 home win over Coventry City and in 434 League and Cup games for the Town, scored fifty two goals with his best season being 1952–53 when he netted eighteen goals in forty five games.

Elsworthy, who was one of the best Welsh wing-halves never to be capped, played the last of his games for the club against Bolton Wanderers on 19 September 1964 before retiring.

EUROPEAN CUP

Ipswich Town's presence in the 1962–63 European Cup was one of football's fairy tales because only five years earlier the Suffolk club had been in the Third Division (South).

On 18 September 1962, Alf Ramsey took Town to Malta for a preliminary round game against Floriana. The islanders were completely outclassed as Ray Crawford and Ted Phillips scored two goals apiece in the club's 4–1 win. The game at Portman Road was even more one-sided. Ipswich helped themselves to a 10–0 victory as Ray Crawford netted five of the goals, Phillips and Moran two each and Elsworthy one. The club looked forward to the first round proper and the Italian champions, Inter Milan.

In the first leg in the San Siro Stadium, Ipswich found themselves two goals down in the opening quarter of an hour before Brazilian striker Sani scored a third on the hour. In a match played in pouring rain, on a pitch littered with puddles, Town almost pulled a goal back in the last minute when Stephenson hit the Inter Milan post with a free kick.

In the return leg at Portman Road, Phillips missed an easy opportunity in the opening minutes and both he and Stephenson had hit the post before half-time. Bill Baxter also hit the Inter Milan woodwork with a rasping free–kick but it was the Italian side who took the lead against the run of play when Barison scored his third goal of the tie. With ten minutes to play, Crawford equalised and then in the eighty fourth minute, Stephenson beat two defenders before shooting against the bar. However, on this occasion the ball dropped to Blackwood who scored from close range. Ipswich had won 2–1 but lost 4–2 on aggregate.

EUROPEAN CUP WINNERS' CUP

Ipswich travelled to Holland to play AZ67 Alkmaar for their first match in the competition on 13 September 1978 and produced a fine rearguard action to draw 0–0. In the return leg at Portman Road a goal from Paul Mariner and a penalty converted by John Wark took Town through to the second round where they were drawn against Austrian club SW Innsbruck.

In a hard fought first leg at Portman Road, John Wark scored the only goal of the game from the penalty spot. The second leg in Austria looked to be heading for a goal-less draw but with just fifteen minutes to go, Innsbruck scored to take the game into extra time. George Burley scored in the 100th minute and although Town had Paul Mariner sent off for a second bookable offence, they held on to win 2–1 on aggregate.

In the quarter-final, Ipswich drew Barcelona and although Eric Gates scored two goals for the Portman Road club, the Spanish side scored an away goal. In the second leg, Barcelona scored the only goal of the game to go through on the 'away goals' rule. They then went on to win the trophy, beating Fortuna Dusseldorf 4–3 after extra–time in the final.

EVER–PRESENTS

There have been thirty eight Ipswich Town players who have been ever-present throughout a Football League season. The greatest number of ever-present seasons by an Ipswich player is seven by Mick Mills. Next in line is Bill Baxter with four.

F

FA CUP

IPSWICH Town first participated in the FA Cup in October 1890 when they beat Reading 2–0 at Portman Road. In the second qualifying round, they beat Norwich Thorpe 4–0 before disposing of Huntingdon County in the next round 5–2. In the fourth and final qualifying round, Town lost 4–1 at home to the 93rd Highlanders. The next two seasons of FA Cup football saw the club knocked out on each occasion by Old Westminsters. This last defeat in 1892–93 was the club's last FA Cup match until 1930–31 when the Blues decided to enter the competition again instead of the Suffolk Senior Cup.

In 1936–37 the club, playing in the Southern League for the first time, recorded some big victories in the FA Cup – Eastern Company United 7–0, Stowmarket 8–0 and Cromer 11–0, as well as beating Football League opposition in Watford 2–1 before losing 2–1 at home to Spennymoor United in the second round.

Town had a good FA Cup run in 1953–54, the season in which they won the Third Division (South) championship. Despite conceding a penalty in under a minute of their first round match against Reading, they came back strongly to win 4–1. Drawn against Walthamstow Avenue, one of the leading amateur teams of the day in the second round, Town were held to a 2–2 draw at Portman Road. In the replay a goal by Alex Crowe settled the tie in Ipswich's favour after the former St Mirren player had been left out of the first match. In round three, Ipswich were held to a 3–3 draw at home to Oldham Athletic before a Tom Garneys goal gave Town a 1–0 win at Boundary Park after England international George Hardwick had missed a penalty for the Lancashire club. A Billy Reed goal was enough to defeat Birmingham City in the fourth round. For the fifth round, Town were drawn away to First Division Preston North End. A Deepdale crowd of 34,500 saw Tom Finney turn on the style as the Lilywhites beat the Suffolk club 6–1.

The club had little success in the competition although they did reach the fifth round again in 1970–71 after replay wins over Newcastle United and West Bromwich Albion. In the fifth round, an outstanding display by Geoff Hammond enabled the club to get a goal-less draw at Stoke City's Victoria Ground but in the replay the Potters won 1–0 with Dennis Smith scoring the goal.

In 1974–75 Town reached the semi-finals of the FA Cup for the first time. After beating League Cup holders Wolverhampton Wanderers 2–1 in round three, Ipswich beat FA Cup holders Liverpool 1–0 at Portman Road with Mick Mills the goalscorer. In the fifth round, the Blues found themselves 2–0 down to Aston Villa but a goal from David Johnson and two from substitute Bryan Hamilton took the club into the quarter-finals for the first time. Ipswich's opponents were Leeds United who played out a goalless draw at Portman Road. The replay at Elland Road also ended all square, at 1–1 after extra time, before Town won the third meeting between the clubs 3–2. In the semi-final, the club played West Ham United at Villa Park. An injury hit Ipswich side held on for a goal-less draw but in the replay at Stamford Bridge, the Hammers won 2–1.

In 1977–78, Ipswich won the FA Cup for the only time in their history. After a 2–0 win over Cardiff City at Ninian Park, Fourth Division Hartlepool United were beaten 4–1 at Portman Road to set up a fifth round meeting with Bristol Rovers. On an icy Eastville pitch, the Blues were grateful to come away with a 2–2 draw. In the replay the club won comfortably 3–0 and travelled to Millwall for the sixth round tie. In a one-sided affair, Paul Mariner scored four goals as the Blues won 6–1 at The Den. In the semi-final, Town beat West Bromwich Albion 3–1 at Highbury with goals from Talbot, Mills and Wark. In the final, a goal from Roger Osborne was enough to beat favourites Arsenal 1–0 and so take the FA Cup back to Suffolk for the first time.

The club reached the semi-final stage again in 1980–81. Aston Villa were beaten 1–0 in the third round with Paul Mariner scoring for the Blues, but in the fourth round, Ipswich were held to a goal-less draw at Gay Meadow before they beat Shrewsbury 3–0 at Portman Road. The club continued to a keep a clean sheet in defeating Charlton Athletic 2–0 before the sixth round saw the Blues drawn away to Nottingham Forest. In a superb cup tie, Ipswich drew 3–3 at the City Ground before an Arnold Muhren goal settled the tie in Town's favour in the replay. In the semi-final, Ipswich lost 1–0 after extra time to Manchester City in a closely fought game at Villa Park.

The club's best performance in recent years was to reach the sixth round in 1992–93 where they lost 4–2 at home to Arsenal.

FEENEY, JIM

Full-back Jim Feeney joined Ipswich from Swansea Town with fellow Irish international Sam McCrory for a combined fee of £10,500 in March 1950.

He made his debut for the Portman Road club in a 1–1 draw at Carrow Road in the East Anglian derby, just a few days after joining the club and over the next six seasons was a virtual ever-present in the Ipswich side. In 1953–54 he missed just two matches as the Blues won the Third Division (South) championship and the following season was outstanding in the Ipswich defence even although the club were relegated from the Second Division.

One of the most popular of Town players, he played the last of his 232 League and Cup games at Brighton in September 1956. Sadly he suffered a broken nose in the sixth minute, reducing the club to ten men.

FERGUSON, BOBBY

Bobby Ferguson came from a footballing family, his father having played for West Bromwich Albion and his uncle for Chelsea. A tough-tackling defender, he began his career with Newcastle United but after making only eleven appearances in seven years with the Magpies, left to join Derby County in 1962. He became a first team regular at the Baseball Ground, making 121 League appearances in little over three years.

On New Year's Eve 1965, he joined Cardiff City and soon settled in to give the Bluebirds three years good service. When he was released he joined Barry Town as player/manager before coming back into league football with Newport County. He had a fairly torrid time at Somerton Park and when he was dismissed in 1971, he linked up with Bobby Robson at Ipswich eventually graduating to the manager's post at Portman Road when Robson became England supremo.

In 1984–85 Ipswich reached the sixth round of the FA Cup and the semi-finals of the League Cup but the following season they were relegated. In

1986–87 Ferguson took the club to fifth place in the Second Division but after the club lost to Charlton Athletic in the play offs, Ferguson had the sad distinction of being the first manager to be sacked by Ipswich Town.

FEWEST DEFEATS

During Ipswich's Second Division championship winning season of 1967–68, the club went through the forty two match programme losing only five games. The first of these came in the sixth game of the season at Blackburn Rovers (1–2) after the club had won two and drawn three of the first five fixtures. At the beginning of December 1967, the club lost three matches in succession – Queen's Park Rangers (away 0–1), Portsmouth (home 1–2) and Middlesbrough (home 1–2). The club's last defeat that season was at Carlisle United on 10 February when they went down 4–1. Ipswich then proceeded to win ten and draw five of their remaining games to win the championship with fifty nine points, one ahead of Queen's Park Rangers and Blackpool.

FIRST DIVISION

Ipswich Town have had three spells in the First Division, although their

Ipswich Town's First Division team of 1976–77.

48

last one followed the reorganisation of the Football League in 1992–93.

After winning the Second Division championship in 1960–61, Town went on to win the League Championship in their first season in the top flight with Ray Crawford top-scoring with thirty three goals including a hat-trick in a 5–2 home win over Chelsea. Two seasons later the club finished bottom of the First Division and were relegated.

The club returned to the top flight after winning the Second Division championship in 1967–68 and spent the next eighteen seasons in the First Division. During this spell, the club finished runners-up in season's 1980–81 and 1981–82 and finished third on three occasions. Relegated in 1985–86, the Blues won promotion to the Premier League in 1991–92 before dropping down to the First Division in 1994–95.

The club have now spent three seasons in their third spell in the First Division, winning play-off places in 1996–97 and 1997–98.

FIRST LEAGUE MATCH

Ipswich Town played their first Football League match on Saturday 27 August 1938 when Southend United were the visitors to Portman Road. A crowd of 19,242 saw Town take a second minute lead through Fred Jones to put them on the way to a 4–2 win. Other scorers were Gilbert Alsop, Bryn Davies and Jones again in what was a comfortable victory.

The Ipswich side that day was: Mick Burns; Billy Dale; Ossie Parry; George Perrett; Tom Fillingham; Jimmy McLuckie; Jackie Williams; Bryn Davies; Fred Jones; Gilbert Alsop and Jackie Little;

FIRST MATCHES

The club's opening match was a practice game played on Broom Hill on 26 October 1878 between the 'Secretary's Team' and the 'Club'. The president, T C Cobbold MP, not only presented the club with a new ball but actually played in the game. The result was a 2–2 draw which was quite remarkable, considering that the secretary's team only had seven players compared to the club's twelve .

The following week the club beat Stoke Wanderers also at Broom Hill 6–1. The outcome was hardly a surprise as the visitors did not know the rules and had not played the game before .

FLOODLIGHTS

Portman Road switched on its floodlights for the first time on 16 February 1960 with a friendly against Arsenal. Ipswich won 4–0 with goals by Phillips, Crawford (2) and Millward.

Each floodlight tower was 110 feet high and held thirty lights. The total cost of £15,000 was paid by the Supporters' Association. The switching on ceremony was performed by Lady Blanche Cobbold, mother of the then chairman 'Mister John' and widow of 'Captain Ivan'.

FOOTBALL LEAGUE CUP

Sad to relate, with the exception of the seasons of 1981–82 and 1984–85 when the club reached the semi-final stage of the competition, Ipswich have made little impact upon the Football League (later Milk, Littlewoods, Rumbelows, Coca Cola and Worthington) Cup.

Entering the competition for the first time in 1960–61, the Blues were beaten 2–0 at home by Third Division Barnsley .In 1961–62 the club had a little more success. They beat Manchester City 4–2 Swansea Town 3–2 after the first game had ended all square at 3–3 and Aston Villa 3–2 before losing 4–1 at Blackburn Rovers.

In view of their European commitments, the club decided not to enter the League Cup the following season but then when they did return in 1963–64, they went out in the first round to Walsall. Town did reach the fifth round in 1965–66 and in 1967–68 beat Southampton 5–2 with Ray Crawford scoring four of the goals. The following season the club lost 4–2 at home to Norwich City in the first League Cup meeting between the sides.

In 1981–82 Town reached the semi-final of the League Cup for the first time. After beating Leeds United in both legs of the second round tie, the Blues disposed of Bradford City after a replay before winning 3–2 at Everton. Drawn at home to Watford in the fifth round, goals from Wark and Brazil took them through to the two-legged semi-final against Liverpool. Despite having a lot of the game, Town lost 2–0 at home to the Reds in the first leg and although Brazil and Gates gave the club some pride back in a 2–2 second leg draw at Anfield, it was never going to be enough.

The club reached the semi-final stage for a second time in 1984–85.

After beating Derby County 4–1 in the first leg of the second round tie, a Mich D'Avray goal at the Baseball Ground gave them a 1–1 draw and a third round tie at home to Newcastle United. A late equaliser by Eric Gates salvaged a draw for Town who then went on to win 2–1 in the replay at St James' Park. After beating Oxford United 2–1 in round four, the club needed two matches to defeat Queen's Park Rangers and win a place in the semi-finals. Paired with arch rivals Norwich city, a Mich D'Avray goal gave Ipswich a 1–0 lead to take to Carrow Road for the second leg. Sadly, in a very physical game, Town lost 2–0 to a Canaries side that went on to lift the trophy.

The club's best scoreline in the competition is 6–1 when they beat Swindon Town in November 1985. Mick Mills and John Wark both appeared in forty four League Cup ties and Wark scored thirteen goals.

FOOTBALLER OF THE YEAR

The Football Writers' Association Footballer of the Year award for 1981 was won by Frans Thijssen, who became the first foreigner to win it since Manchester City's Bert Trautmann in 1956. Mick Mills was second in the poll with John Wark, third.

That same season, the Professional Footballers' Association award for Player of the Year went to John Wark.

FOREIGN OPPOSITION

Town's first match against foreign opposition took place on 18 November 1891 when they entertained the Canadian and American Tourists at Portman Road. The club had to guarantee their visitors £20 although the money taken at the gate did not cover this amount. The tourists had already beaten a number of professional sides, so it was something of a surprise when Ipswich won 2–1.

FORMATION

Although Ipswich Town were only admitted to the Football League in 1938, the club was formed at a meeting held in the Town Hall on 16 October 1878 when T C Cobbold MP was elected president.

Originally it was the Ipswich Association FC to distinguish it from the other Ipswich Football Club which played rugby. In 1888 these two amalgamated and the handling game was dropped five years later.

FORREST, CRAIG

Vancouver-born goalkeeper Craig Forrest joined Ipswich as an apprentice in September 1984 and signed professional forms just under a year later but when he was unable to claim a first team place he was loaned out to Colchester United. He made his Football League debut for the Layer Road club against Wrexham in March 1988.

The following season he started as the club's first choice 'keeper and played in the first twenty two games until he was deemed at fault for all of the goals in a 3–0 defeat at Chelsea. Ron Fearon displaced him but Forrest worked hard at his game and won his place back. He was an ever-present in 1989–90 and continued to impress the following season as he reaped the benefit of the club's specialist goalkeeping coaching provided by Phil Parkes. In 1991–92 he was again ever-present as Town won the Second Division championship and earn automatic promotion to the Premier League.

Forrest was also selected for the Canadian national team after the season had ended but his first season in the Premiership was ruined by injury and suspension. His suspension came following being sent off in the second minute of the home game against Sheffield United for 'serious foul play'. He thus became the first Ipswich goalkeeper ever to be sent off in the Football League.

Despite the emergence of Richard Wright, Forrest who has been capped forty five times by Canada went on to play in 314 first team games for the club before leaving Portman Road to join West Ham United.

G

GARNEYS, TOM

TOM GARNEYS joined the club from Brentford in the summer of 1951 and made his debut in the opening game of the 1951–52 season, scoring in a 4–1 defeat of Southend United. He ended the season with twenty League and Cup goals to top the club's scoring charts – a feat he achieved in five of his eight seasons at Portman Road. In 1953–54 he scored nineteen goals in forty four league games to help the Blues win the Third Division (South) championship and the following season, despite missing half the campaign with a bad injury, netted twenty goals in twenty four games, including four in a 5–1 win over Doncaster Rovers. Garneys had just returned after a four match absence and was playing against doctor's orders. It was the first time that an Ipswich player had scored more than three goals in a Football League match.

In 1955–56 he scored a hat-trick in a 5–0 win at Northampton Town but despite scoring nineteen goals in thirty six league games, it was the first season that he had not finished as the club's leading scorer. In 1957–58 he was back to his best and topped the scoring charts with nineteen goals in thirty three games. However, the following campaign was to be Tom Garneys last, for in January 1959, having scored 143 goals in 274 games for the Portman Road club, he retired from the game to run the Mulberry Tree Inn in Ipswich.

GATES, ERIC

Although Eric Gates made his Ipswich Town debut as a substitute for Roger Osborne in a 2–0 home win over Wolverhampton Wanderers on 27 October 1973, it was 4 October 1975 before he made his full first team debut in a 1–0 defeat at Derby County after having made thirteen appearances as a substitute.

All Eric Gates' football with the Portman Road club was played in the First Division, although it was 1977–78 before he established himself as a first team regular.

Two seasons later, Gates, pictured left, netted his first hat-trick for the club in a 4–0 home win over Manchester City. In the previous game at Portman Road, his strike in Ipswich Town's 3–1 defeat of Southampton had been selected as *Match of the Day's* Goal of the Month for November 1979.

Gates continued to find the net over the next two seasons in which Town finished runners-up in the First Division on both occasions.

His form led to him winning two full caps for England, his first in the World Cup qualifying match against Norway at Wembley in 1981. Injuries hampered his progress in 1982–83 but in 1983–84, he was the club's top scorer with sixteen goals including a hat-trick in the 3–0 third round FA Cup win at Cardiff City.

Gates was the club's leading scorer again in 1984–85 but at the end of that season, the Ferryhill-born player, who had scored ninety six goals in 384 first team outings, left Portman Road to join Sunderland.

At Roker Park, Gates scored forty three goals in 181 League games before leaving the Wearsiders to end his career with Carlisle United.

GOALKEEPERS

Ipswich Town FC has almost always been extremely well served by its goalkeepers and most of them have been popular with the club's supporters.

The club's first goalkeeper in the Football League was Mick Burns who had played for Preston North End in the FA Cup Final of 1937. He went on to make 168 League and Cup appearances. Jack Parry, who won one Welsh cap when with Swansea Town, joined the club in 1951 and was ever-present in 1953–54 when Ipswich won the Third Division (South) championship.

Roy Bailey arrived at Portman Road in March 1956 and made his debut in the East Anglian derby against Norwich City. He proved to be a great servant, making 345 League and Cup appearances in his eight years with the club. Former Port Vale 'keeper Ken Hancock was ever-present in season's 1966–67 and 1967–68 when the club won the Second Division championship. David Best, who conceded the 'goal that never was', made 199 appearances for the Portman Road club following his arrival from Oldham Athletic in 1968. Laurie Sivell spent fourteen seasons at Ipswich, most of the time as understudy to Paul Cooper, but he still managed to appear in 175 first team games. Penalty saving expert Cooper appeared in a total of 572 games during his twelve seasons as the club's first choice 'keeper.

The club's present goalkeeper is Richard Wright, who has been called up to the England Under-21 and B sides, and it is surely only a matter of time before he wins full international honours.

GOALS

The most goals Ipswich Town have ever scored in one game is eleven, a feat achieved on two occasions – Languard Fort 11–1 in the Suffolk Senior Cup semi-final of 1895–96 and Cromer 11–0 in the third qualifying round of the FA Cup in 1936–37.

The club have scored ten goals on six occasions, the latest being the 10–0 European Cup victory over Maltese side Floriana in September 1962 when Ray Crawford netted five of the goals. In the Football League, the most goals scored by the club is seven. Town have won three matches by a 7–0 scoreline – against Portsmouth in 1964–65, Southampton in 1973–74 and West Bromwich Albion in 1976–77.

GOALS – CAREER BEST

The highest goalscorer in the club's history is Ray Crawford who between season 1958–59 and the end of season 1968–69 had netted 227 goals for Ipswich. These comprised of 204 in the league, five in the FA Cup, ten in the League Cup and eight in Europe.

GOALS – INDIVIDUAL

Only two players have scored five goals in a game since the club were elected to the Football League in 1938–39. The first was Ray Crawford who netted five in Town's 10–0 European Cup win over Floriana at Portman Road on 25 September 1962. Alan Brazil scored all the club's goals in a 5–2 home win over Southampton on 16 February 1982, including a five minute hat-trick.

On 30 October 1880, John Knights scored nine goals in the club' biggest win, 15–0 against East Samford, and Alfred Arthur Green – never known as anything else except 'Dammo' – scored eight goals in a 10–0 Southern Amateur League win over Eastbourne on 30 April 1932.

GOALS – SEASON

The club's highest league goalscorer in any one season remains Ted Phillips who scored forty one league goals as Ipswich won the Third Division (South) championship in 1956–57. Netting hat-tricks against Queen's Park Rangers (home 4–0) and Watford (home 4–1) he also scored five goals in three FA Cup appearances.

GOALSCORING RECORDS

Ipswich Town are the only Football League club which has had three players who all scored as many as four times in a European Cup match.

Trevor Whymark achieved the feat on two occasions in the UEFA Cup against Lazio in 1973–74 and Landskrona in 1977–78. Ray Crawford actually scored five against Floriana in the 1962–63 European Cup and John Wark had four against Aris Salonika in the 1980–81 UEFA Cup when the club went on to win the trophy.

GRASS ROOTS

Ipswich Town did not lose at home in the 1953–54 season until 23 January 1954, some supporters putting their run of success down to a seven leaf clover given to them by a fan from America .

GREEN, 'DAMMO'

Local stonemason Alfred Arthur Green, who was always known as 'Dammo', was the club's goalscoring sensation in the pre–league days.

Possessing a powerful shot, he played his first game for the club on 16 November 1929, scoring a goal in Town's 2–0 win over Aquarius in the Southern Amateur League. He ended that first season with twenty three goals in twenty one games, including netting hat-tricks against Eastbourne (home 6–1) and London Welsh (home 9–2), as Town won the League Championship.

Eastbourne certainly suffered at the hands of 'Dammo' for the following season he scored four goals against them in a 6–2 win and in 1931–32, netted a remarkable eight goals in a 10–0 thrashing.

During his time at Portman Road, he won three Southern Amateur League championship medals and scored 129 goals in 146 games.

GUEST PLAYERS

The guest system was used by all clubs during the two wars. Although at times it was abused almost beyond belief – in that on occasions some sides that opposed Ipswich during the 1945–46 season had ten or eleven guests – it normally worked sensibly and effectively to the benefit of players, clubs and supporters alike.

Among the guests to turn out for Ipswich that season were Biggs from Aberdeen, Parlane from Glasgow Rangers, Harris from Watford and Gillespie from Crystal Palace.

H

HAMILTON, BRYAN

BRYAN HAMILTON was already a Northern Ireland international when he joined Ipswich Town from Linfield in the summer of 1971 for a fee of £20,000.

He made his debut in a goal-less draw at home to Everton on the opening day of the 1971–72 season and although he only played in a handful of matches during that campaign, he was ever-present and joint top scorer with eleven league goals in 1972–73. The following season he was the club's leading scorer with sixteen goals in forty one games as Town finished fourth in Division One. He netted his only hat-trick for the club in March 1975 as Newcastle United were beaten 5–4 at Portman Road.

He had scored fifty six goals in 199 first team games when he left Ipswich to join Everton for £40,000.

He played for the Goodison Park club in the League Cup Final of 1977, although he will always be remembered on Merseyside for scoring 'the goal that never was'. In the FA Cup semi-final against Liverpool, the game stood at 2–2 when with just seconds remaining, Hamilton hammered the ball past the despairing dive of Ray Clemence to apparently clinch Everton's place at Wembley. For no reason whatsoever, referee Clive Thomas ruled out the Irishman's effort and Liverpool went on to win the replay 3–0.

He later played for Millwall and Swindon Town before joining Tranmere Rovers as player/manager. Sacked in 1985, he then led Wigan Athletic to Wembley success in the Freight Rover Trophy Final before taking charge at Leicester City. He returned to Springfield Park in 1988 but lost his job in 1993 as the Latics struggled to get away from the foot of Division Two.

Capped fifty times for Northern Ireland, he became the national manager until replaced by Lawrie McMenemy in 1998.

HANCOCK, KEN

Goalkeeper Ken Hancock had five years as an amateur with Stoke City but when they failed to offer professional terms he joined Port Vale and after making his debut in a 4–2 defeat at Millwall on 13 December 1958, he was ever-present during the rest of Vale's 1958–59 Fourth Division championship season. He spent six years with Vale and made 269 League and Cup appearances before signing for Ipswich Town for a fee of £10,000 in December 1964.

He conceded four goals on his Ipswich debut as the Blues lost 4–1 at Preston North End. However, he proved himself a reliable, clean-handling and competent 'keeper and in the seasons of 1966–67 and 1967–68 he was ever-present, playing in 108 consecutive League and Cup games. In the 1967–68 season, Hancock kept twelve clean sheets and made a number of memorable saves as the club won the Second Division championship.

He later played for Tottenham Hotspur, Bury, Stafford Rangers and Northwich Victoria before returning to Port Vale as part-time coach and standby goalkeeper. However, it was discovered because he had received a pay out from the provident fund, he could not play for the club and he moved to become the player/coach and later manager of Leek Town.

HARPER, COLIN

Local-born left-back Colin Harper played his first game for the club in a 3–0 defeat at Plymouth Argyle in February 1966 but it was another four seasons before he established himself as a first team regular. He was one of only two ever-presents in 1971–72 and scored his first league goal for the Town the following season in a 4–1 home win over Manchester United.

Haper was often under-rated and his Portman Road career was hampered by injuries and he was restricted to 168 League and Cup games in thirteen years with the club.

After playing his last game for the Blues in December 1974, in a fifth round League Cup tie at Carrow Road which ended 1–1, he had loan spells at Grimsby Town and Cambridge United before joining Port Vale as player/coach in July 1977.

He was appointed acting manager three months later but departed at the end of November as the new manager, Bobby Smith, brought in his own staff. He then had a spell with Chelmsford City before becoming player/manager to Sudbury Town.

HAT-TRICK HEROES

Ipswich's first hat-trick in the Football League was scored by Ambrose Mulraney in the 4–0 win over Bristol City on 8 April 1939.

In 1955–56, Wilf Grant scored two Football League hat-tricks against Millwall as Town won 6–2 at home and 5–0 at The Den. He also scored three goals that season against Reading but his record was beaten the following season by Ted Phillips who scored five hat-tricks in the Football League as Town won the Third Division (South) championship.

The only occasion when two Ipswich players have scored hat-tricks in the same match came in the game against Sunderland at Portman Road on 19 September 1958. Town won 6–1 with Dermot Curtis scoring the first three goals and Ted Phillips, who netted eight hat-tricks in his Ipswich career, the last three.

Gerry Baker is the only Town player to score a hat-trick and finish on the losing side. He did this at White Hart Lane on 4 April 1964 as the Blues lost 6–3 to Tottenham Hotspur.

Colin Viljoen scored a hat-trick on his Ipswich debut on 25 March 1967 in a 4–2 home win over Portsmouth after the Fratton Park club had been two goals up inside the first quarter of an hour.

John Wark became the first man to score a hat-trick of penalties in European competition when three of his four goals against Greek side Aris Salonika came from the spot in a first round UEFA Cup match in 1981. In total, Wark scored a record fourteen goals in Ipswich's eventually successful cup run. The only other Ipswich player to score a hat-trick of penalties was George Perrett in the second qualifying round of the FA Cup against Lowestoft Town at Portman Road on 21 October 1936.

One of the quickest hat-tricks scored by an Ipswich player was by Alan Brazil for the visit of league leaders, Southampton, on 16 February 1982. Brazil scored his hat-trick in the space of five minutes – at the 14th, 17th and 19th minutes – and went on to net all five in Town's 5–2 win.

Ray Crawford holds the club record for most hat-tricks scored with ten, including five goals in the match against Floriana and four in the League Cup against Southampton.

HEGAN, DANNY

Born in Coatbridge, Danny Hegan began his career with Albion Rovers before moving into the Football League with Sunderland. Unable to break into the first team at Roker Park, he joined Ipswich in September 1963 and made his debut in a 6–0 defeat by Bolton Wanderers at Burnden Park .

Over the next six seasons, Hegan was a virtual ever-present in the Ipswich side and in 1967–68 missed just one game as the club won the Second Division championship.

It was during the 1968–69 season, when the club were back in the top flight, that he began to feel he was getting into a rut. Although he was born in Scotland, Hegan had an Irish father and his outstanding displays brought him very close to full international honours for Northern Ireland. He was on the transfer list for a number of months before in the 1969 close season, he was allowed to join West Bromwich Albion in exchange for Ian Collard, who was valued at £60,000, and a cheque for £30,000.

Hegan, who scored thirty eight goals in 234 League and Cup games for Ipswich, won the first of seven international caps for Northern Ireland while at The Hawthorns when he played against USSR in 1970.

He later played for Wolverhampton Wanderers before returning to the north east to end his league career with Sunderland.

HOME MATCHES

Ipswich Town's best home win is the 10–0 rout of Floriana in the preliminary round of the European Cup on 25 September 1962. They have scored seven goals in a Cup or League match at Portman Road on six occasions – Street (FA Cup in 1938–39, 7–0) Aldershot (Division Three South in 1938–39, 7–2), Portsmouth (Division Two in 1964–65, 7–0), Southampton (Division One in 1973–74, 7–0), West Bromwich Albion (Division One in 1976–77, 7–0) and Skeid Oslo (UEFA Cup 7–0).

HOME SEASONS

Ipswich Town have never gone through a complete league season with an undefeated home record. The nearest they came to it was in 1955–56 when they lost just one game at Portman Road, 2–0 against Torquay United on the opening day of the season.

HONOURS

The major honours achieved by the club are:

First Division Championship	1961–62
Second Division Championship	1960–61, 1967–68, 1991–92
Third Division(S) Championship	1953–54, 1956–57
FA Cup	1977–78
UEFA Cup	1980–81
Texaco Cup	1972–73

HUNDRED GOALS

Ipswich Town have scored more than 100 League goals in a season on three occasions. The highest total is 106 goals scored in 1955–56 when they finished third in Division Three (South). The following season they scored 101 goals in winning the Third Division (South) title with Ted Phillips scoring forty one goals in forty one appearances. The last time the club scored 100 goals was in 1960–61 when they won the Second Division championship.

The club have conceded over 100 league goals on just one occasion and that was in 1963–64 when they let in 121 goals in and finished bottom of the First Division. Their defeats that season included Fulham (away 1–10) Stoke City (away 1–9) Manchester United (home 2–7) Bolton Wanderers (away 0–6) Arsenal (away 0–6) Liverpool (away 0–6) and Tottenham Hotspur (away 3–6).

HUNTER, ALLAN

Northern Ireland international centre-half Allan Hunter began his career with Coleraine, for whom he played in the European Cup Winners' Cup before entering the Football League with Oldham Athletic in January 1967. After eighty three league appearances for the Boundary Park club he joined their Lancashire neighbours Blackburn Rovers for a fee of £30,000 in the summer of 1969. He had a similar playing record with the Rovers and after appearing in eight four league games left Ewood Park to join Ipswich Town in September 1971.

After making his debut alongside Derek Jefferson in the heart of the Ipswich defence in a 2–1 home defeat by Leicester City, Hunter went on to play in all the remaining twenty five league games of that 1971–72 campaign. Although he was never ever-present, he formed a fine partnership with Kevin Beattie and missed very few matches over the next seven seasons.

During his time at Portman Road, Hunter, who was voted the club's Player of the Year in 1975–76 was hailed as the best centre-half in the Football League.

The winner of 53 full caps for Northern Ireland, forty seven of them when with Ipswich, he left the club in April 1982 after amassing 355 first team appearances to become player/manager at Colchester United.

The genial Irishman did not relish the managerial side of the game and after only eight months in charge, he resigned. Four years later, he returned to Layer Road as coach.

I

INTERNATIONAL PLAYERS

IPSWICH TOWN'S most capped player (ie: caps won while players were registered with the club) is Allan Hunter with forty seven caps. The following is a complete list of players who have gained full international honours while at Portman Road.

England		Northern Ireland	
Kevin Beattie	9	Bryan Hamilton	21
Terry Butcher	45	Allan Hunter	47
Ray Crawford	2	Pat Sharkey	1
Eric Gates	2	Kevin Wilson	3
David Johnson	3	**Scotland**	
Paul Mariner	33	Alan Brazil	11
Mick Mills	42	George Burley	11
Russell Osman	11	John Wark	26
Brian Talbot	5	**Wales**	
Colin Viljoen	2	Mick Hill	2
Trevor Whymark	1	Cyril Lea	2
Republic of Ireland		William Reed	2
Tommy Carroll	8		
Kevin O'Callaghan	17		

Ipswich's first player to be capped was William Reed when he played for Wales against Scotland in 1955.

IPSWICH HOSPITAL CUP

The club reached the final of this competition on seven occasions, winning the trophy three times – King's Lynn 1–0 in 1929–30; King's Lynn 1–0 in 1930–31 and Harwich and Parkeston 1–0 in 1932–33. From 1936–37 the club opposed Football League clubs in the final with the following results:

1936–37 Norwich City 3–2, 1937–38 Queen's Park Rangers 4–3, 1938–39 Aston Villa 2–3, 1939–40 Crystal Palace 0–4, 1946–47 Norwich City 1–2, 1947–48 Chelsea 3–0 and 1948–49 West Ham United 2–0.

J

JEFFERSON, DEREK

DEREK JEFFERSON made his first team debut for Ipswich Town in an FA Cup third round tie against Shrewsbury Town on 28 January 1967 as a replacement for the injured Bill Baxter. Although it was his only appearance that season, he established himself in the heart of the Ipswich defence in 1967–68 and gave the club good service over the next six seasons.

In 1968–69, Jefferson made more first team appearances than any other player and scored his only goal for the club in a 2–2 draw at Tottenham Hotspur. That season also saw Jefferson become the first player to be sent off at Portman Road and only the second in a Football League match when he received his marching orders in a 3–1 home defeat by Chelsea on Boxing Day 1968.

Jefferson went on to play in 175 League and Cup games for the Blues before Bobby Robson agreed to transfer him to Bill McGarry's Wolverhampton Wanderers for a fee of £88,000 in October 1972.

After a loan spell at Sheffield Wednesday he left Molineux to end his league career with Hereford United.

JOHNSON, DAVID

David Johnson joined Everton in 1969 but despite scoring fifteen goals in fifty eight appearances including a hat-trick in an 8–0 win over Southampton, he was allowed to join Ipswich Town for a fee of £100,000 in October 1972.

He made his debut the following month in a 2–2 home draw against Leeds United and became an instant hit with the Town supporters. Forming a fine understanding with Trevor Whymark he went on to score forty six goals in 178 games including a hat-trick in a 4–0 home win over Coventry City on 16 November 1974.

It was while he was at Portman Road that he won the first of his eight

full international caps for England when he played against Wales in 1975. However, the following year he left Ipswich to become Liverpool's first £200,000 signing.

Not helped by a succession of injuries, he managed only glimpses of his best form and although he collected a title medal and figured in the Wembley defeat by Manchester United, he missed out on European glory.

He helped to win a second League Championship medal in 1978–79 but in August 1982, after netting seventy eight goals in 204 games, he returned to Everton for £100,000.

His second spell at Goodison was little short of a disaster as his goal touch was missing. He had a loan spell at Barnsley before joining Manchester City. He then had a brief spell with the NASL side,Tulsa Roughnecks, before ending his league career with Preston North End.

David Johnson, pictured left, occupies a unique place in Merseyside folklore, being the only man to score a derby winner for both Everton and Liverpool.

JOHNSON, GAVIN

A hard-working midfielder, he was given his chance in 1988–89, making his league debut at Portman Road in the number three shirt against Barnsley on 21 February 1989, just a few days after signing professional.

Although he only played in a handful of games over the next couple of seasons, he performed well when he was required. Johnson finally came to the fore in 1991–92, appearing in most of the club's games when they won the Second Division championship. In fact, it was his goals in the last two games of the season which clinched the Championship.

He made a great start to the 1992–93 season when he scored the club's first goal in the new Premier League with a 30 yard shot high into the roof of the Aston Villa net. At the end of the season, Johnson's goal was named by the Supporters' Club as their 'Goal of the Season'.

He had made 159 first team appearances for the Portman Road club when, in the 1995 close season, he was given a free transfer and joined Luton Town. However, his stay at Kenilworth Road was short and in December 1995 he was

Gavin Johnson at work in mid-field for Wigan Athletic.

transferred to Wigan Athletic for £15,000 where he remains an important member of the club's first team squad.

JUBILEE FUND

The League Benevolent Fund was launched in 1938, fifty years after the start of the Football League to benefit players who had fallen on hard times.

It was decided that the best way to raise funds was for sides to play local derby games with no account being taken of league status. own visited Norwich City on 17 August 1938 where a Carrow Road crowd of almost 18,000 saw the teams play out a 1–1 draw. In the return match at Portman Road at the start of the following season, Town ran out winners 2–1 in what was to stand as the club's only competitive match of the season.

K

KENT, ERNEST

AFTER attending Kesgrave Hall School, where his father was the head-master, Ernest Kent worked as an apprentice printer, although still finding time to play for both Ipswich and Suffolk County.

He played at either inside or centre-forward and appeared in more than 200 games, including friendlies, and scored well over 200 goals.

He was the first Ipswich Town player to receive a testimonial for his services when in April 1903 a match between the club's side of that year and the team of 1895–96 took place. Fittingly, Kent scored for his side with a powerful strike.

When he died, aged ninety one, in 1960 his ashes, by special arrangement with the Portman Road club, were scattered on the pitch.

KIWOMYA, CHRIS

An athletic striker with great pace, Chris Kiwomya followed his brother Andy into league soccer when he joined Ipswich Town as a trainee in the summer of 1986. On turning professional, he had to wait a further eighteen months before making his league debut as a substitute at Portman Road against Bradford City on 24 September 1988.

Despite showing some early promise, he did not really become a regular until 1990–91 when he played in thirty four matches and topped the club's goalscoring charts. When he arrived at Portman Road, he was a winger but was converted by Town manager, John Lyall, into a central striker. Surprisingly overlooked for England Youth and Under-21 honours, he was a regular in the Ipswich side as they won the Second Division championship in 1991–92, leading the way with sixteen league goals, plus another three in cup competitions.

He made quite an impact in the new Premier League with his pace and in the 4–0 League Cup victory over Wigan Athletic, he scored his first hat-trick for the club.

Although he was the club's leading league goalscorer for three consecutive seasons from 1990–91 to 1992–93, his all-round confidence and ability in front of goal seemed to have disappeared when Arsenal manager George Graham paid £1.25 million, a figure set by a tribunal, to take Kiwomya to Highbury in January 1995.

At the end of that season he had scored three goals in fourteen league appearances but he was never to appear in the Gunners' first team again. Beset by injuries and a loss of form he had a loan spell with French club Le Havre before starting the 1998–99 season with Queen's Park Rangers.

Chris Kiwomya in action against Nottingham Forest

69

L

LAMBERT, MICK

MICK LAMBERT, who had the honour of being twelfth man for England in the 1969 Lord's Test match against the West Indies, worked his way up  through the club's ranks before making his first team debut in a goal-less draw at home to Coventry City in March 1969.

Over the next few seasons, Lambert found himself in and out of the Ipswich side before replacing Jimmy Robertson for the club's 1972–73 First Division campaign. The winger then missed very few games over the next four seasons and in 1975–76 scored his only hat-trick for the club in a 3–1 FA Cup third round win over Halifax Town. Lambert went on to score forty five goals in 263 games for the club before leaving Portman Road in July 1979 to join Peterborough United.

At London Road, Lambert scored two goals in twenty one league games for 'Posh' before injury forced him to retire from league football.

LARGEST CROWD

It was on 8 March 1975 that Portman Road housed its largest crowd. The occasion was the FA Cup sixth round match against Leeds United. A crowd of 38,010 saw Ipswich play out a goal-less draw against the Elland Road side. The clubs went on to meet four times before Ipswich won 3–2 at Filbert Street.

LATE FINISHES

Ipswich's final match of the season against Northampton Town at the County Ground on 31 May 1947 is the latest date for the finish of any of the club's Football League campaigns. A crowd of 3,200 saw Stan Parker and George Clarke score for Ipswich in a 2–2 draw.

LEA, CYRIL

Originally a full-back, Cyril Lea's career blossomed when he was converted to wing-half. He established himself in Leyton Orient's team from 1960–61 and went on to make 205 league appearances for the Brisbane Road club. He helped the Os into the First Division in 1962 but after losing his place, he joined Ipswich Town in November 1964.

After making his first team debut in a 1–1 home draw against Charlton Athletic, he plaed in the remaining twenty four games of the season, captaining the side on six occasions. His form was such that season, that he was capped twice by Wales at full international level, against Northern Ireland in Belfast and Italy in Florence.

Appointed club captain, he missed very few games over the next two seasons, the latter of which saw Town finish fifth in Division Two. In 1967–68 when Town won the Second Division championship, Lea made just four appearances and only one as substitute the following season when the club were in the top flight.

Lea had played in 123 games for the Blues and on retiring, joined the club's coaching staff, although he did have a short spell as caretaker manager when Frank O'Farrell left the club.

He later coached the Welsh national side and was assistant to Alan Durban at Stoke City. Lea also had three good seasons at Colchester United when they just missed promotion in each of the campaigns he was in charge, yet surprisingly, despite his relative success, he was sacked.

LEADBETTER, JIMMY

Jimmy Leadbetter began his football career with his home club, Edinburgh Thistle, before joining Chelsea in the summer of 1949. Unable to make much of an impression at Stamford Bridge, only appearing in three league games, he moved to Brighton and Hove Albion where over the next three seasons, at either inside-forward or left-wing, he scored twenty nine goals in 107 league games.

He signed for Ipswich in July 1955 and made his debut for the Blues in a 1–0 home win over Bournemouth on 8 October 1955. After that, he was one of the first names to be pencilled in on the club's team sheet and was an ever-present in the seasons of 1957–58, 1959–60 and 1960–61. He played in 138 consecutive league matches between 11 October 1958 and 23 December 1961 and was one of only five players to win Championship medals for all three division with the same club.

He went on to score forty nine goals in 375 League and Cup games for the club, with his best season being 1956–57 when the club won the Third Division (South) championship. He left the club at the end of the 1964–65 season to play non-league football for Sudbury Town.

LEADING GOALSCORERS

Ipswich Town have provided the Football League's leading divisional goalscorer on three occasions:

1956–57	Ted Phillips	Division Three(South)	41 goals
1960–61	Ray Crawford	Division Two	39 goals
1961–62	Ray Crawford	Division One	33 goals

LEAGUE GOALS – CAREER HIGHEST

Ray Crawford holds the Portman Road record for the most league goals with a career total of 204 goals between 1958 and 1969.

LEAGUE GOALS – LEAST CONCEDED

During the 1976–77 and 1979–80 seasons, Ipswich conceded just 39 goals when finishing third in the First Division in both campaigns.

LEAGUE GOALS – MOST INDIVIDUAL

Ted Phillips holds the Ipswich Town record for the most league goals in a season with forty one scored in just forty one Third Division (South) games in 1956–57.

LEAGUE GOALS – MOST SCORED

Ipswich Town's highest goals tally in the Football League was in the 1955–56 season when they scored 106 goals in finishing third in the Third Division (South).

LEAGUE VICTORY – HIGHEST

Ipswich Town's best league victory is 7–0, a scoreline achieved on three occasions. The first came on 7 November 1964 in a Second Division clash with Portsmouth. Joe Broadfoot opened the scoring after just 31 seconds and Frank Brogan netted his first hat-trick for the club. On 2 February 1974, Southampton were beaten in a First Division match at Portman Road and the club received £250 from the *Sun* newspaper for being the first top flight club to score seven goals that season.

The last occasion Ipswich won 7–0 in the Football League was against West Bromwich Albion on 6 November 1976 when Trevor Whymark scored four of the goals.

LINIGHAN, DAVID

The son of Brian, who played for Darlington in 1958 and like his brother Andy, who also joined Hartlepool United from Smiths Dock, he made his league debut at home to Bradford City in March 1982. For a long while he played mainly in the shadow of Andy and it was not until 1985–86 that he held down a regular place.

He impressed Arthur Cox enough for Derby County to pay £30,000 for his services but after just four months and no first team appearances, he was sold to Shrewsbury Town. He missed only three matches in eighteen months at Gay Meadow and with Ipswich looking to replace Ian Cranson following his move to Sheffield Wednesday, they signed Linighan for a fee of £300,000.

He soon became a fixture in central defence and in 1990–91 he had an outstanding season as the club's captain, which was recognised by the Ipswich faithful when he picked up the fans 'Player of the Year' award. Linighan also played a sterling role in the Blues Second Division championship campaign in 1991–92 until he was injured in the home game against Barnsley which ruled him out for the rest of the season.

He went on to maintain a high level of defensive consistency in the Premier League and had played in 327 first team games for the Blues before joining Blackpool for £80,000 in November 1995 after an extended loan spell with the Seasiders.

LITTLE, JACKIE

Gateshead-born forward Jackie Little joined the club as an amateur in 1935 and made his debut in a 3–1 home win over Gorleston in an Eastern Counties League game on 14 September 1935. It was not until the 1937–38 season that he established himself as a first team regular and in what was the club's last season in the Southern League, he scored eleven goals in twenty eight games including a hat-trick in the 3–1 home win over Tunbridge Wells Rangers.

He appeared in the club's first match in the Football League, a 4–2 defeat of Southend United and went on to score six goals in thirty two games that season. During the war, he guested for Bath City where he played alongside the Blackpool and England forward Stan Mortensen. When league football resumed in 1946–47, Little was still a member of the Town side and went on to score twenty goals in 146 Football League games for the club before at the end of the 1949–50 season, leaving Portman Road to become player/manager of Stowmarket.

LONG SERVICE

John Cavendish Cobbold was club chairman from 1957 to 1976, and managers Scott Duncan and Bobby Robson both gave long service. On the playing side, John Wark in three spells with the club, between 1974 and 1996 appeared in 681 first team games. Other players to have given the club long service include Mick Mills (1966–1982); Paul Cooper (1974–1987); George Burley, the club's present manager (1973–1985); Bill Baxter (1960–1971); and Tommy Parker (1946–1957).

LOWE, DAVID

Coming from a family with a typical northern passion for the game, David Lowe's early football was restricted to school and local league level. His teacher recommended him to Wigan Athletic's Harry McNally and he was soon offered an apprenticeship. However, injuries to first team regulars forced the club to take a calculated risk and play him against Reading in October 1982. Although his inexperience showed, the Latics stuck with him and over the next five seasons, he made 231 appearances, scoring fifty three goals.

In June 1987 he signed for Ipswich Town for a fee of £80,000 and made his debut in a 1–1 draw at home to Aston Villa on the opening day of the 1987–88 season. He ended the campaign as the club's top scorer with seventeen goals in forty one games.

The hard-working midfielder won England Under-21 honours and continued to find the net for the Portman Road club. He was the leading scorer again in 1989–90 but two seasons later found himself on loan at Port Vale. He left Ipswich in the summer of 1992 when Leicester

David Lowe.

City paid £250,000 for the services of a player who had scored forty five goals in 159 first team games.

At Filbert Street he soon became a first team regular and popular with the fans for his wholehearted approach but after another loan spell with Port Vale, he was allowed to leave and rejoin Wigan Athletic for £125,000 in March 1996.

The Springfield Park favourite has since set up a new club aggregate scoring record after topping the scoring charts in 1997–98 when he was also voted Player of the Year. In his two spells with the Latics, Lowe has scored eighty goals in 335 first team games.

LOWEST

The lowest number of goals scored by Ipswich town in a single Football League season is thirty two in 1985–86 when the club were relegated from the First Division.

The club's lowest points record in the Football League occurred in 1963–64 when they gained just twenty five points and were relegated to the Second Division after finishing bottom of the First Division. In 1994–95 when the club ended the season at the foot of the Premier League, they totalled twenty seven points but if that record had been under the old two points for a win system, they would have only totalled twenty points.

LYALL, JOHN

As a player, John Lyall represented England Youth against Luxembourg at Upton Park in 1957 and was a member of the West Ham side beaten by Manchester United in the FA Youth Cup Final later that year. Sadly, Lyall was hampered by injuries and was only able to make thirty one league appearances before eventually conceding defeat in the summer of 1963.

He worked in the offices at Upton Park for a while before taking up coaching at the club. In 1971 he became assistant manager to Ron Greenwood and then team manager with Greenwood as general manager in August 1974. Lyall was given full managerial responsibilities when Greenwood became England's manager in 1977.

During Lyall's management, the Hammers won the FA Cup twice. In 1975 they beat Fulham 2–0 and in 1980 beat Arsenal 1–0. West Ham also reached the European Cup Winners' Cup Final where they lost 4–2 to Anderlecht in the Heysel Stadium. The club were relegated in 1978 but in 1980–81 they won the Second Division championship and the League Cup Final but lost to Liverpool in a replay.

After the Hammers were relegated again in 1988–89, Lyall, who was the longest-serving manager in the Football League, was sacked.

After working as a technical co-ordinator with Tottenham Hotspur, he was appointed manager of Ipswich Town.

He quickly rebuilt the team and the Portman Road club won the Second Division title in 1991–92. He remained in charge of team affairs until December 1994 when he moved upstairs to become the club's general manager.

═══════M═══════

MALCOLM, KEN

ABERDONIAN Ken Malcolm joined Ipswich from Arbroath in May 1954 and although he was not in the side for the opening game of the season, he had not long to wait before making his debut, playing in the 4–2 defeat at Hull City on 4 September 1954.

Despite only playing in twenty one league games that season due to a niggling groin injury, he showed his versatility by turning out in eight different positions .

At the start of the 1955–56 season he established himself at left-back and over the next eight seasons played in 291 League and Cup games for the Portman Road club, winning a Third Division championship winners' medal in 1956–57 and a Second Division championship winners' medal in 1960–61.

In 1961–62, when Ipswich won the First Division championship, Malcolm only played in three matches because he strained a knee and was later hospitalised for a lengthy time with a bad attack of sciatica.

Although he returned to first team action the following season, it proved to be his last in the Football League, Malcolm not appearing in the Town side again after the 6–1 defeat at West Bromwich Albion on 9 March 1963. During the close season he retired from the playing side of the game and coached the club's juniors for two years.

MANAGERS

The following is a complete list of Ipswich Town's full-time managers together with the inclusive dates for which they held office.

Mick O'Brien	1936–1937	Bobby Robson	1969–1982
Scott Duncan	1937–1955	Bobby Ferguson	1982–1987
Alf Ramsey	1955–1963	John Duncan	1987–1990
Jackie Milburn	1963–1964	John Lyall	1990–1994
Bill McGarry	1964–1968	George Burley	1994–

MARATHON MATCHES

In 1974–75, Ipswich reached the sixth round of the FA Cup for the first time in their history where their opponents were Leeds United. A record crowd of 38,010 watched the first meeting at Portman Road which ended goal-less. In the first replay at Elland Road, the home side's equaliser came in the third minute of injury time. The club's then played out another goal-less draw at Filbert Street before Ipswich won the third replay 3–2 with Clive Wood's winning goal being voted the BBC's 'Goal of the Month'. The four matches took a total of seven hours of play before the tie, which was watched by 142,849 spectators, was settled.

MARINER, PAUL

Paul Mariner began his footballing career with non-league Chorley before being transferred to Plymouth Argyle for a small fee in July 1973. Within weeks of the start of the 1973–74 season he had displaced Jimmy Hinch and became recognised as one of the leading forwards in the Third Division and his scoring partnership with Billy Rafferty did much to ensure Argyle's promotion to the Second Division in 1975–76. It also attracted the attention of First Division clubs, Ipswich, West Bromwich Albion and West Ham United but it was Bobby Robson who made the Home Park club an offer they could not refuse in October 1976. With seven goals in ten league games, Mariner had already demonstrated that he could get goals in the Second Division as well as the Third and Argyle accepted Ipswich's valuation of the player – £220,000 including two Town players, Terry Austin and John Peddelty.

Mariner made his Ipswich debut in a 1–0 win at Manchester United and had a hand in the club's goal scored by Clive Woods.

Robson's high opinion of Mariner continued after the former had left Ipswich to become manager of the national team and Mariner was awarded the first of his thirty five caps some six months after moving to Portman Road.

In his first season with the club, he scored thirteen goals in thirty one League and Cup games including a hat-trick in a 4–1 home win over West Ham United. In 1977–78 he was the top scorer with twenty two goals including another hat-trick in a 6–1 sixth round FA Cup win at Millwall.

He ended the campaign with an FA Cup winners' medal after the Blues had beaten Arsenal 1–0 in the final. He led the scoring charts again in 1978–79 and 1979–80 and in this latter season, netted his third hat-trick for the club in a 6–0 win over Manchester United. Although his goalscoring achievements were less over his last three seasons at Portman Road, he had scored 131 goals in 339 League and Cup games when he signed for Arsenal in February 1984 for £150,000.

Although hardly in the veteran stage, he had seen his best years and in August 1986 after scoring seventeen goals in seventy first team games for the Gunners, he joined Portsmouth. In his first season at Fratton Park he helped the club gain First Division recognition for the first time in almost thirty years. He later had a brief spell as commercial manager of Colchester United but now spends most of his time coaching in the United States.

Paul Mariner.

MARKSMEN – LEAGUE

Ipswich Town's top league goalscorer is Ray Crawford who struck 204 league goals during his Portman Road career. Only four players have hit more than 100 league goals for the club.

1	Ray Crawford	204	7	Trevor Whymark	75
2	Ted Phillips	161	8	Eric Gates	73
3	John Wark	135	9	Alan Brazil	70
4	Tom Garneys	123	10=	Gerry Baker	58
5	Paul Mariner	96		Frank Brogan	58
6	Tommy Parker	86			

MARKSMEN – OVERALL

Six players have hit a century of goals for Ipwich Town. Top marksman is Ray Crawford. The Century Club consists of:

1	Ray Crawford	227
2	John Wark	182
3	Ted Phillips	179
4	Tom Garneys	143
5	Paul Mariner	135
6	Trevor Whymark	104

MARSHALL, IAN

He began his career with Everton and made his league debut when deputising for the injured Derek Mountfield against West Bromwich Albion at Goodison Park in August 1985. However, first team chances were few with Kevin Ratcliffe and Dave Watson holding down the central defensive positions and so in March 1987 he moved to Oldham Athletic for a fee of £100,000.

On his arrival at Boundary Park he tried to convince Oldham manage,r Joe Royle, that there was a frustrated centre-forward in him trying to get out. Royle did indeed try him up front during the club's great twin cup runs of 1989–90 with some success. But after scoring in the first FA Cup semi-final against Manchester United in 1990, he was injured and missed selection for the League Cup Final against Manchester United in 1990. In 1990–91 he scored a superb hat-trick in a 3–2 win at Wolverhampton Wanderers and ended the season as the club's top scorer with seventeen goals from only twenty six league games as Oldham stormed to the Second Division championship. During the inaugural season of the Premier League, he played in thirteen games up front and thirteen at the back. With no one seeming to know what his best position was, he joined Ipswich Town for a fee of £750,000 in the summer of 1993.

He proved his worth as a striker with three goals in the opening three matches of the 1993–94 campaign and ended the season as the club's top scorer. He was hampered by injuries the following season but in 1995–96 he notched up nineteen goals, the same number as his strike partner, Alex Mathie, even though he helped out in defence on a number of occasions.

His classic header against Leicester City earned him the club's 'Goal of the Season'. He had scored thirty seven goals in ninety six League and Cup games for Ipswich when in August 1996 he left Portman Road to join newly promoted Premier League club, Leicester City, for £800,000.

MASON, PAUL

Although he was born in Liverpool, he started his career in mainland Europe and continued it in Scotland before entering league football in England with Ipswich ten years later.

He was signed as an associate schoolboy by Everton but left Goodison without being offered an apprentice ship by the club. After playing non-league football on Merseyside, he went to work in Holland where he was discovered by Groningen FC when playing for a works side. After five seasons of playing in Dutch football, he signed for Aberdeen in the summer of 1988.

He spent another five years at Pittodrie, winning a Skol Cup winners' medal in 1989 when he scored both goals in a 2–1 extra–time win over Rangers. He had scored thirty seven goals for the Dons in 192 first team outings when in the summer of 1993 he joined Ipswich Town for a fee of £400,000.

He made his debut against Oldham Athletic on the opening day of the 1993–94 season, scoring the club's last goal in a 3–0 win. Although he can play up front, Mason prefers a wide role, which allows him to cut in looking for the shot. He was the club's top scorer in 1996–97 with fifteen League and Cup goals and although a broken hand kept him out for most of 1997–98 he has, albeit belatedly, forged a reputation in English football.

McCALL, STEVE

After making his first team debut against Skeid Oslo in the UEFA Cup first round first leg tie in Norway, midfielder McCall played his first league game three days later in a 1–1 draw at home to Everton. Never a prolific scorer in his time at Portman Road, he netted two of Town's goals in the return leg against Skeid Oslo which the Suffolk club won 7–0.

After winning a regular place in the Ipswich side in 1980–81, McCall was capped by England at Under-21 level to add to those he won at youth

Steve McCall.

level. He went on to play in six internationals at Under-21 level before being chosen for the England B team in 1984–85.

In 1981–82 he was one of four ever-presents in the Ipswich side as they finished runners-up to Liverpool in the First Division. In fact, McCall played in every league game for the next two seasons, appearing in 166 consecutive games.

On 13 April 1985 he broke a bone in his foot in the 2–1 home defeat by Sheffield Wednesday and had to miss the rest of the season. He bounced back in 1985–86 and went on to score eleven goals in 329 first team games before being transferred to Sheffield Wednesday for £300,000 in the summer of 1987.

At Hillsborough he suffered with injuries and a loss of form and in almost five years with the Yorkshire club, only appeared in thirty six first team games. In March 1992 he joined Plymouth Argyle for £25,000 and spent four years at Home Park, playing in 117 games before becoming player/coach at Torquay United.

McCRORY, SAM

Belfast-born centre-forward Sam McCrory began his footballing career with Linfield before Swansea Town brought him into league football. In three seasons at the Vetch Field he scored forty six goals in 103 League games and helped the Swans win promotion to the Second Division.

He arrived at Portman Road in March 1950 along with Irish international full-back Jim Feeney for a combined fee of £10,500, a record for Ipswich. He made his debut in a 1–1 draw at Norwich City but before the end of the season he had the dubious distinction, in a 5–0 defeat at Aldershot, of becoming the first Ipswich player to be sent off since the club joined the Football League.

In 1950–51 he was the club's top scorer with twenty one league goals including a hat-trick in a 3–1 win at Crystal Palace. He headed the scoring charts again the following season with sixteen goals but in the summer of 1952 he joined newly-promoted Plymouth Argyle.

Never an automatic choice at Home Park, his career was revived somewhat after his transfer to Southend United in 1955 and at the age of thirty three he received his sole international cap for Northern Ireland, scoring in a rare win over England in 1957.

McGARRY, BILL

Discovered by Port Vale in 1945, he moved to Huddersfield Town for a fee of £12,000 in March 1951. He soon established himself in the First Division and in 1954 he won the first of four England caps when he played in the World Cup Finals in Switzerland. He was also capped for England B, played for the Football League and went on the FA's 1956 South African tour. He scored twenty six goals in 381 League and Cup games for the Yorkshire club before becoming Bournemouth's first player/manager. From July 1963 he was the manager of Watford and in October 1964 he moved to Ipswich Town as manager.

Remembered for his competitiveness as a player, he carried that approach into his managerial career and at Portman Road he concentrated on building up the players' strength and stamina. In only his sixth game in charge, the club recorded their highest victory in a league match when they beat Portsmouth 7–0.

In 1967–68 he took the club to the Second Division championship but in November 1968 he moved to Wolverhampton Wanderers and led them into Europe where they reached the final of the UEFA Cup. He also led them to success in the 1974 League Cup Final before being sacked in May 1986 after the club had been relegated.

He later coached in Saudi Arabia and managed Newcastle United. There followed spells as Brighton scout, Power Dynamo (Zambia) coach, Zambian national team manager and periodic coaching in South Africa before he spent sixty one days in a second spell managing Wolves. Disillusioned he quit the game before returning to South Africa to coach Bopnutbuswanana.

McLUCKIE, GEORGE

Falkirk-born winger George McLuckie began his career with Lochore Welfare before coming south of the border to play for First Division Blackburn Rovers. He had scored two goals in twenty league appearances for the Ewood Park club when Scott Duncan signed him for Ipswich Town during the summer of 1953.

He made a goalscoring debut in the opening game of the 1953–54 season, a 2–0 win at Walsall and went on to be one of five ever-presents as

Town won the Third Division (South) championship. While laying on a number of goals for leading scorer, Tom Garneys, the dangerous winger bagged twelve himself to finish third in the club's scoring list.

Liking nothing better than to cut inside from the left-wing and test the opposing goalkeeper, McLuckie scored twenty five goals in 152 League and Cup appearances. He left Portman Road in June 1958 and joined Reading where he played in eighty five league games for the Elm Park club.

McLUCKIE, JIMMY

Jimmy McLuckie was a Scottish international, being capped against Wales in 1934 when he was a Manchester City player. When he joined Ipswich from Aston Villa in July 1936, he was the biggest name so far to join the Portman Road club.

He was Ipswich's first professional captain and made his debut in a 4-1 home win in the club's first Southern League fixture of 1936–37 and went on to score five goals in twenty seven games as Town won the League Championship. The following season he scored four goals in thirty two games as Ipswich finished third in the Southern League and then in 1938–39 guided the club into their first season in the Football League. Leading by example, he missed just one game as the club finished in a very creditable seventh position.

During the war years, he was one of a number of Ipswich players who guested for Norwich City but in 1945–46, when the football authorities decided to operate some organised leagues, he appeared in seventeen games, the last against Watford on 13 April 1946.

Having played an important part in the development of the professional club at Ipswich, he left to become manager of Clacton Town.

McNEIL, MICK

Mick McNeil began his league career with his home club, Middlesbrough, and made his debut against Brighton and Hove Albion during the 1958–59 season. He soon established himself at full-back, the position in which he would be capped for England. He was selected for an FA XI against the Army at Newcastle and followed this up with a number of appearances for the England Under-23 side.

He made an impressive debut against France at Roker Park and then went on tour to East Germany, Israel and Poland. McNeil was a forceful defender who could carry the ball through to set up attacks and eventually, his gritty displays earned him his full England debut in Belfast. Eight further caps quickly followed but in the summer of 1964 after he had made 193 first team appearances for the Teeside club, he joined Ipswich Town.

He made his debut for the Portman Road club in a goal-less draw at Cardiff on the opening day of the 1964–65 season and over the next seven years went on to play in 173 League and Cup games. Although he did not add to his collection of international caps, he captained an FA XI to a 10–0 win over Jersey, played to commemorate the centenary of the Jersey FA.

He played his last game for the Blues in a 1-0 fourth round FA Cup defeat at Birmingham City in February 1972 before entering non-league football with Cambridge City.

MILBURN, JACKIE

'Wor Jackie' was an idol of the Geordies for over a decade and was without doubt, one of the best centre-forwards in the Football League after the Second World War. Fast and with a lethal shot, he scored a number of spectacular goals including two in Newcastle's 1951 FA Cup Final success over Blackpool. In 1955 he scored one of the quickest-ever Wembley goals after just 45 seconds of the Magpies' 3–1 win over Manchester City. He scored 199 goals in 395 games for Newcastle before moving to Linfield where he led the side to two Irish Cup Finals.

He returned to England as player/coach at Southern League Yiewsley under Bill Dodgin before succeeding Alf Ramsey as manager of Ipswich Town in January 1963.

He inherited quite an old squad at Portman Road and in a season in which they conceded 121 goals including a 10-1 defeat against Fulham, the club finished bottom of the First Division with only twenty two points and nine wins. He continued to have a difficult time at the start of the 1964–65 season and his health began to suffer. On 4 September he tendered his resignation and entered the newspaper world. He remained for more than twenty years years covering north-eastern football from the press box. When he died of cancer in 1988, the whole of Newcastle city centre ground to a halt for his funeral.

MILLS, MICK

Mick Mills began his career with Portsmouth but was released when the Fratton Park club abandoned their youth policy. Ipswich Town snapped him up and it was not long before he made for his league debut on 7 May 1966 against Wolverhampton Wanderers in a match that Ipswich won 5–2. Just over three years later he became the first player in Ipswich history to make 100 league appearances before his twenty first birthday.

Following Bill Baxter's departure midway through the 1970–71 season, Mills was appointed the club captain and over the next twelve years led the Blues by example. It was 1973, when his name was extremely well-known around England's big grounds as a full-back or midfield player of non-stop momentum and perception, that he was called up for the national side for the first time when he played against Yugoslavia.

It was a high personal honour when he captained his country for the first time against Wales at Cardiff in 1978, but his proudest moment was to lead England against the challenge of Switzerland in a World Cup eliminator at Wembley in 1980.

An unobtrusive yet inevitable part of the England defensive set up, Mills won forty two caps, his last against Spain in 1982.

For Ipswich he was ever-present in four successive seasons from 1972–73, appearing in 198 consecutive league games. Known as 'Captain Fantastic', the highlights of his career were the winning of the FA Cup in 1978 when Arsenal were beaten 1–0 and the defeat of AZ67 Alkmaar in the final of the UEFA Cup in 1980–81.

Mills, who appeared in 741 first team games, a club record, left Portman Road in November 1982 to join Southampton for a fee of £50,000. He soon fitted in to the Saints style of play and over the next three seasons played in 121 League and Cup games including being ever-present in 1984–85 when the club finished fifth in the First Division.

In the summer of 1985 he moved to Stoke City as player/manager but after a number of mediocre seasons, he was replaced by Alan Ball whom he had recently appointed as his assistant. He also managed Colchester United and had a spell as assistant manager at Coventry City.

MILTON, SIMON

Simon Milton joined Ipswich Town fromm local Eastern Counties League club, Bury Town in the 1987 close season and made his league debut while on loan with Exeter City at home to Stockport County in November 1987, scoring two goals. He was soon back at Portman Road but another loan spell at Torquay United followed before he returned to Ipswich to play in the club's last six games of the season. In the final match of the campaign, he scored the winning goal in a 3–2 win at Bradford City which lifted Town three places in the Second Division to eighth.

Over the next few seasons, Milton proved himself capable of scoring explosive goals after bursting through from midfield, even though he was extremely unfortunate with injuries. He also showed his versatility, play-ing wide on the right, in central midfield and as a ball winner. He was voted the supporters 'Player of the Year' in 1995–96, and was given a free transfer at the end of the 1997–98 season after having appeared in 332 first team games for the Blues.

MORRIS, PETER

Peter Morris began his league career with Mansfield Town where his manager was the legendary Raich Carter. He made his debut for the Stags on 24 February 1961 at Workington when only seventeen and a year later he was made the captain. He went on to score fifty goals in 287 League games for Mansfield before in March 1968 he joined Ipswich Town for a fee of £12,000.

He made his debut for the Blues in a fine 3–2 win over Derby County and played in the last fourteen matches of the club's Second Division championship winning season. In 1972–73, Ipswich won the Texaco Cup with Morris scoring both goals in the 2–1 first leg win over Norwich City at Portman Road. Also that season, his well judged long passes helped the club finish fourth in the First Division and so qualify for Europe. With young talent such as Beattie and Mills coming through at Portman Road, Morris who had scored sixteen goals in 258 first team games, left to join rivals Norwich City for £60,000.

After a couple of seasons at Carrow Road, he turned down manager John Bond's offer of a player/coach position to manage Mansfield Town where he took his total league appearances for the Field Mill club to 328. He later managed Peterborough United and Southend United. After spells coaching in Saudi Arabia and with Leicester City, he managed Kettering Town, where he gave them four years of FA Cup runs and almost a place in the Football League when they finished runners-up in the Conference in 1988–89.

MOST GOALS IN A SEASON

When Ipswich finished third in the Third Division (South) in 1955–56, they scored 106 goals in forty six matches with Tommy Parker the top scorer with thirty. They beat Sindon Town and Millwall 6–2 and Walsall 5–2, all the matches being played at Portman Road. They also scored five goals in three of their away matches, winning at Reading 5–1, Northampton Town 5–0 and Millwall 5–0.

MOST MATCHES

Ipswich played their most matches, sixty six, in season of 1980–81. They comprised forty two league games, seven FA Cup, five Football League

Cup games and 12 UEFA Cup games when they won the trophy.

MUHREN, ARNOLD

A classy midfielder, Dutch international Arnold Muhren began his career with the great Ajax team of the 1970s and was substitute for them in the European Cup Finals of 1972 and 1973, although he never came on in either game. He moved to Twente Enschede before joining Ipswich Town for £165,000 in August 1978.

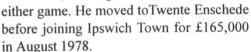

After missing the opening game of the 1978–79 season, he made his first team debut for the Portman Road club in a 3–0 home defeat by Liverpool and went on to score eight goals in forty one league games. He was a great favourite with the Town fans but not before the club had altered their style of play. There was now a lot more variety in the approach with many moves being built up through Muhren in midfield as well as the club's previous moves which were often based on the long ball game. Not surprisingly he ended the season as the supporters choice as 'Player of the Year'.

Muhren returned to Holland in 1981 to collect a UEFA Cup winners' medal with Ipswich but when his contract at Portman Road expired in the summer of 1982, he moved to Manchester United. The popular Dutchman had scored twenty nine goals in 214 first team outings.

At the end of his first season at Old Trafford, he helped United to victory in the FA Cup Final replay against Brighton, scoring a second half penalty. He was hit by injuries towards the end of the 1983–84 season and his demise coincided with the Reds dropping out of the Championship race.

Thereafter, he struggled to find a first team place and in June 1985 he returned to Ajax and appeared in the 1987 Cup Winners' Cup Final. He was also in the Dutch side that captured the 1988 European Championshop but announced his retirement from international football after the final.

MYLES, NEIL

Falkirk-born Neil Myles joined Ipswich Town from Third Lanark in August 1949 and scored two goals on his debut on 24 December 1949 as the Blues drew 4–4 at home to Crystal Palace. During his first three seasons with the club, he played in just twenty games, scoring eight goals from a variety of forward positions. He was then converted to wing-half and was an ever-present over the next two seasons, going on to appear in 110 consecutive league games.

When Ipswich won the Third Division (South) championship in 1953–54, Myles was a key member of the side as he was three seasons later when the club won the championship for a second time.

He went on to score eighteen goals in 245 League and Cup games for the Blues, making his last appearance at Villa Park in September 1959. At the end of that season, Myles left Portman Road to play non-league football with Clacton Town.

N

NELSON, ANDY

HIS displays for London and Essex youth sides persuaded West Ham United to sign Andy Nelson as a professional in 1953. After nearly six years at Upton Park in which he made just fifteen league appearances, he moved to Ipswich Town for £8,000.

He made his first team debut in a disastrous 4–1 home defeat by Huddersfield Town on the opening day of the 1959–60 season and went on to be one of four ever-presents in a side that finished eleventh in the Second Division. The following season he was a leading figure in the Town side that scored 100 goals in winning the Second Division championship and in 1961–62 was again ever-present in the Ipswich team that won the League Championship. Although he never scored a goal for the Blues, the popular centre-half made 215 League and Cup appearances before joining Leyton Orient in September 1964. He had two seasons at Brisbane Road before moving to Plymouth Argyle for a fee of £4,000 in 1965. He was just one short of 100 appearances for the Home Park club when he ended his playing career.

He was later manager of Gillingham and Charlton Athletic.

NEUTRAL GROUNDS

Portman Road has been used as a neutral ground for cup matches on a number of occasions and Ipswich Town have had to replay on a neutral ground a number of times in the FA Cup.

Date	Opponents	Venue	Stage	Score
21.01.1952	Gateshead	Bramall Lane	Round 3(2R)	1–2
01.12.1953	Bournemouth	Highbury	Round 1(2R)	3–2
15.01.1961	Luton Town	Highbury	Round 3(2R)	5–1
25.03.1975	Leeds United	Filbert Street	Round 6(2R)	0–0
27.03.1975	Leeds United	Filbert Street	Round 6(3R)	3–2

The club's FA Cup semi-finals were of course played on neutral grounds:

Date	Opponents	Venue	Score
05.04.1975	West Ham United	Villa Park	0–0
09.04.1975	West Ham United	Stamford Bridge	1–2
08.04.1978	West Bromwich Albion	Highbury	3–1
11.04.1981	Manchester City	Villa Park	0–1

The club's FA Cup Final appearance at Wembley also qualifies for inclusion.

NICKNAME

Ipswich's nickname is either 'Blues' or 'Town'.

NON-LEAGUE

Non-league is the shorthand term for clubs which are not members of the Football League. Below is the club's record in the FA Cup against such opposition:

Date	Opposition	Venue	Score
10.12.1949	Chelmsford City	Away	1–1
14.12.1949	Chelmsford City	Home	1–0
29.11.1951	Merthyr Tydfil	Away	2–2
05.12.1951	Merthyr Tydfil	Home	1–0
12.12.1953	Walthamstow Avenue	Home	2–2
16.12.1953	Walthamstow Avenue	Away	1–0
08.01.1955	Bishop Auckland	Home	2–2
12.01.1955	Bishop Auckland	Away	0–3
19.11.1955	Peterborough United	Away	1–3
17.11.1956	Hastings United	Home	4–0
09.01.1960	Peterborough United	Home	2–3
13.01.1973	Chelmsford City	Away	3–1

NORFOLK AND SUFFOLK LEAGUE

The Norfolk and Suffolk League was formed in the summer of 1897 although it was 1899–1900 before Ipswich Town competed in it. The club's first league match saw them entertain Norwich CEYMS. The game ended 1–1 with Town captain Henman equalising towards the end of the

game. After that first season in which the club finished fourth, they participated in the league for eight seasons with a best position of runners-up in
1902–03.

NORWICH CITY

The first meeting between Ipswich Town and Norwich City took place at
Norwich on 15 November 1902 when a goal from Fred Whitham gave the
home side a 1–0 win.

The two clubs first met in the Football League on 2 September 1939 at
Portman Road. The result was a 1–1 draw but the Football League on the
advice of the government decided to close down the competition for the
duration of the Second World War and so the result of the first league
meeting was expunged from official records.

The East Anglian derby matches first began in Division Three (South)
during Ipswich's second season in the Football League and the Portman
Road club made their intentions clear when three goals from Bert Day
and two from Tommy Parker gave them a convincing 5–0 home win, and
a solitary goal by Stan Parker completed the double later in the season.

The Blues went all out for a repeat performance the next year, winning
5–1 at Carrow Road but were beaten 2–1 at home. In 1949–50, Ipswich's
former Irish international winger Jackie Brown scored all the goals in a
3–0 home win and the next year, in the last but one match of the season,
Ipswich ended Norwich's unbeaten home record as Sam McCrory hit two
goals in a 3–1 victory.

Ipswich Town won the Third Division (South) championship in
1953–54 and took three points off their rivals that season but spending
only one season in Division Two, meetings were resumed again in
1955–56 with Ipswich winning 4–1 at home and losing by the odd goal in
five at Carrow Road.

In his second season in charge, Alf Ramsey guided Ipswich back into
the Second Division as champions. The Canaries languished at the foot of
the table with Ipswich comfortably winning the derby matches 3–1 and
2–1.

When Town won the Second Division championship in 1960–61, they
beat fourth placed Norwich over Christmas 3–0 and 4–1 with Ray
Crawford hitting four of the goals and Ted Phillips, two.

One of the most exciting meetings between the clubs occurred at Carrow Road in 1968, when after going two goals down after 28 minutes, a hat-trick from South African-born Colin Viljoen helped the Portman Road club to win a pulsating encounter 4–3.

The first two meetings in the top flight in 1972–73 produced just three goals with a 2–1 win to Norwich being recorded in the second match of the season.

When the two sides met in 1976–77 there was a crowd of 34,000 at Portman Road to witness a hat-trick from Trevor Whymark to earn the Blues a convincing 5–0 victory with the same players completing the double, scoring the only goal of the game at Norwich.

There were plenty of goals during the 1979–80 encounters. The first game took place at Carrow Road where Ipswich turned a 2–1 interval deficit into a 3–3 draw and then won their home game 4–2 with a hat-trick from John Wark, which included two goals from the penalty spot.

This was really the last goal spree until the two clubs met on 21 February 1998 when Town beat the Canaries 5–0 at Portman Road. Alex Mathie netted a hat-trick and Boby Petta scored Town's other two goals.

Mick Mills and Tom Parker have made the most appearances in an East Anglian derby with seventeen, and John Wark is the leading scorer in the meetings with Norwich with seven goals.

The club's league record against the Carrow Road club is:

P	W	D	L	F	A
64	33	9	22	110	66

O'BRIEN, MICK

Mick O'Brien did not play football until he was eighteen years old when his family moved to South Shields from Ireland. He played his early football with Walker Celtic, Wallsend and Blyth Spartans before his progress was interrupted by the First World War. He served in the Army before the war and then in the Navy and Royal Flying Corps during the hostilities.

In 1919, the giant centre-half signed for Brentford but before the year was out, he had played for both Norwich City and South Shields before joining Queen's Park Rangers. The much travelled defender who later played for Leicester City, Hull City, Derby County, Walsall and Norwich

City (again) and Watford, won ten full international caps for Northern Ireland and four for the Republic of Ireland.

When his playing days were over, he became manager of Queen's Park Rangers but after two years in charge during which time there was little money to spend, he left to become assistant manager at Brentford.

In May 1936, O'Brien was appointed as the first manager of Ipswich Town and in his first season in charge he took the club to the Southern League title when they finished five points ahead of Norwich City Reserves. The following year personal problems, including the death of his wife, began to have an effect on him and in August 1937 he left the club, sadly dying three years later.

O'CALLAGHAN, KEVIN

London-born Kevin O'Callaghan made his Football League debut for Millwall in a 4–2 win at Charlton Athletic as a seventeen year old and a year later arrived at Portman Road in Ipswich's biggest ever 'cash only' deal of £200,000. He had been one of the outstanding players in Millwall's youth team and had been capped by the Republic of Ireland at Youth and Under-21 level. O'Callaghan qualified for the Republic by virtue of his father being born there and in 1981 won the first of twenty one caps when he played against West Germany 'B'.

A naturally left-footed winger, he made his Ipswich debut as a substitute for John Wark in a 4–0 win at Everton on 9 February 1980. Over the next six seasons, O'Callaghan appeared in 147 first team fixtures but fifty nine were as a substitute. After being left out of the Ipswich side for a second round second leg Milk Cup tie at Derby County, O'Callaghan asked for a transfer.

After a two month loan spell at Portsmouth, he joined the Fratton Park club on a permanent basis for a fee of £100,000. After only scoring six goals at Ipswich, he found his shooting boots at Portsmouth, scoring twenty goals in 105 matches before returning to end his league career with his first club, Millwall.

OLDEST PLAYER

The oldest player to line up in an Ipswich Town first team is goalkeeper Mick Burns, who was forty three years 219 days old when he played in the

FA Cup third round match against Gateshead (home 2–2) on 12 January 1952.

OSBORNE, ROGER

One of the game's unsung heroes, he made his debut in a 2–0 home win over Wolverhampton Wanderers in October 1973 but then had to wait until the 1975–76 season before establishing himself as a first team regular at Portman Road when he appeared in thirty six games as Town finished sixth in the First Division.

Although never a prolific scorer – finding the net in just ten games in 149 first team appearances – his goal that gave Ipswich a 1–0 FA Cup Final win over Arsenal in 1978 will always endear him to Town fans.

It came in the 77th minute as Geddis' cross was cut out by Arsenal centre-half Willie Young, only for the ball to run loose to Roger Osborne who hit home a left foot shot out of the reach of the Gunners' Irish international 'keeper Pat Jennings. The excitement of scoring proved too much for Osborne and he was replaced immediately by Mick Lambert.

Sadly, Osborne missed the entire 1978–79 season with a knee injury and although he made a handful of appearances over the next couple of seasons, his Portman Road career was over and in February 1981, the club's goalscoring hero left to join Colchester United for a fee of £25,000.

During his eight seasons at the club, he showed his versatility and ability to man mark the opposing team's top player. There is no better example than when he completely marked Johan Cruyff out of the game in a 3–0 home win over Barcelona in the 1977–78 UEFA Cup.

He went on to play in 206 league matches for the Layer Road club before leaving the first class game.

Russell Osman.

OSMAN, RUSSELL

Russell Osman began his Football League career with Ipswich Town where under the managership of Bobby Robson, he formed an excellent central defensive partnership with Terry Butcher. In 1975 he won an FA Youth Cup winners' medal though he had to wait until September 1977 before making his first team debut in a 1–0 home win over Chelsea.

In May 1980 he won the first of eleven full international caps for England when he played against Australia and made his last appearance for his country against Denmark in a European Championship match in September 1983. He twice went close to a League Championship medal – as the club finished runners-up in the First Division in 1980–81 and 1981–82. He also helped them win the UEFA Cup in 1981, when they beat AZ67 Alkmaar 5–4 on aggregate.

Osman was an ever-present in seasons of 1979–80 and 1980–81 and had played in 384 first team games for the club when he left Portman Road in the summer of 1985 to join Leicester City for a fee of £240,000. He made 108 league appearances for the Filbert Street club before signing for Southampton for £325,000 in June 1988.

Osman's first managerial role was with Bristol City where he was initially caretaker manager but in 1994 he lost his job. He became manager of Cardiff City in November 1996 but midway through the following season, he was replaced by Frank Burrows. Osman is now back at Ashton Gate as Bristol City's coach.

OVERSEAS PLAYERS

Probably the first overseas player to represent Ipswich town was William Havenga, a South African forward who joined the club from Luton Town in January 1952. He scored three goals in nineteen appearances before leaving to play non-league football for Kettering just over a year after joining the Portman Road club.

After the 1978 World Cup, Town signed Dutch international midfielder Arnold Muhren from FC Twente for £150,000. He had previously played with Johan Cruyff at Ajax and went on to score twenty nine goals in 214 first team games before joining Manchester United. Later during the 1978–79 season, Dutch international and former team mate of Arnold

Muhren at FC Twente, Frans Thijssen joined the club. The two Dutch players along with Scottish international John Wark formed one of the most successful midfields in the Football League. Thijssen appeared in 170 first team games, scoring sixteen goals, before leaving in April 1985 to play for Vancouver Whitecaps.

Another Dutch international to play for the Blues was Surinam-born Romeo Zondervan who joined the club from West Bromwich Albion and in eight years at Portman Road made 274 league appearances.

Russian international Sergei Baltacha joined the Portman Road club from Dynamo Kiev in January 1989. Other overseas players have included Vlado Bozinoski and Bontcho Gueentchev, who both made their debuts in the club's first season in the Premier League in 1992–93. Guentchev, the first Bulgarian to play in the top flight, went on to score eleven goals in seventy five League and Cup games following his arrival from Sporting Lisbon. Uruguayan Adrian Paz played in just seventeen matches, and Danish international midfielder, Claus Thomsen, made ninety seven first team appearances before joining Everton. Gus Uhlenbeek, who joined Town from Top Ost for £100,000 in the summer of 1995, made 112 appearances before leaving to join Fulham. Niklas Gudmundsson joined Ipswich on loan from Blackburn Rovers and helped them reach the play off finals at the end of the 1996–97 season.

The only two overseas players still on the club's books are Mauricio Taricco and Bobby Petta. Taricco arrived at Portman Road in September 1994 from Argentinos for £175,000 and last season was selected for the PFA Nationwide Division One team. Petta joined the club on a free transfer from Feyenoord and is now beginning to display the form that persuaded manager George Burley to bring him to Portman Road.

P

PARKER, TOMMY

TOMMY PARKER guested for the club in the 1945–46 season when he was in the Navy at Shotley and in the twelve games he played, scored three goals.

He made his league debut in the game against Norwich City on 7 September 1946, scoring two goals in a 5–0 win for the Portman Road club and ended the season with eleven goals in forty games. Having established himself in the Ipswich side, Parker missed just one game in each of season's 1950–51, 1951–52 and 1952–53, before being an ever-present in 1953–54 when the club won the Third Division (South) Championship.

Although he scored his fair share of goals, his most prolific term for the club was 1955–56 when he broke the club's scoring record with thirty goals in the league and another in the FA Cup. His only hat-trick that campaign came in a 6–2 home win over Swindon Town. Remarkably, Parker lost his first team place to Ted Phillips the following season and the Leiston-born forward smashed Parker's scoring record with forty one league goals and five more in the FA Cup.

Parker, who had scored ninety five goals in 475 outings, left Portman Road at the end of that season before returning in 1965 to take charge of the club's Development Association. He finally retired some twenty years later, receiving a watch and a commemorative certificate to mark his loyal service to Ipswich Town.

PARRY, OSSIE

Ossie Parry joined the Blues from Crystal Palace in the summer of 1936, having made 141 League appearances for the Selhurst Park club.

Ipswich's first professional player, he made his debut for the club in a 4–1 home win over Tunbridge Wells Rangers on the opening day of the 1936–37 Southern League season. He went on to appear in all but two of the club's games in that campaign as they won the Southern League

101

Championship. In 1937–38, the strong-tackling full-back was the club's only ever-present as they finished third in their last season in the Southern League. The following season, which was Town's first in the Football League, Ossie Parry and goalkeeper Mick Burns were the only ever-presents as the club finished seventh in the Third Division (South).

Parry's career. like so many others. was hampered by the Second World War, although he did play in thirty one of the matches played in 1945–46 when the Third Division (South) was split into two halves to prevent clubs from having too greater distances to travel.

When football resumed after the hostilities, Parry continued to be an integral member of the Ipswich side, playing the last of his 197 first team games in a 6–1 defeat at Brighton on 7 May 1949 at the age of forty years 264 days.

PENALTIES

Fred Turner scored Ipswich's first penalty on 23 December 1893 in a 7–0 win over Saxmundham. In a match against Leiston on 5 December 1891, a rather curious incident occurred. A Leiston player, thinking that the referee had blown his whistle for an infringement, caught the ball in his hands as it was heading for the goal. Remarkably, the referee believed his explanation and instead of awarding a penalty kick to Town, gave a free kick to Leiston, thus robbing the club of what would have been their first penalty. On 15 October 1898, Claude Woods scored from the spot in Ipswich's 3–1 defeat against Kirkley. He also missed a penalty and this is widely believed to be the first that Town ever missed.

On 23 October 1909, Ipswich played the Casuals at home in a Southern League match. During the course of the game, which the visitors won 4–0, Ipswich were awarded a penalty for hand ball. Bill Double took the spot kick but made no attempt to score, it being the Town players way of indicating that he thought the offence accidental.

During the 1925–26 season, goalkeeper George Harris scored twice fom the penalty spot – a feat only he has achieved.

Five penalty kicks were awarded in the replayed FA Cup tie between Ipswich and Lowestoft Town on 21 October 1936. Ipswich scored all theirs, courtesy of George Perrett. Lowestoft scored one and missed another of their penalties. Ipswich won 7–1 after a 1–1 draw in the second qualifying round.

On 7 January 1939, Ipswich travelled to Villa Park for a third round FA Cup tie. Early in the second half, with the game still goal-less, Town were awarded a penalty. As Charlie Fletcher shaped to take the kick, the Villa 'keeper, Biddlestone, danced up and down on the goal-line and at the last split second before he connected with the ball, it was moved by a piece of mud thrown by Villa full-back Callaghan. The shot hit the post and despite furious protests by the Ipswich players the referee refused to let the kick be re-taken. Villa went on to take the lead before Hutcheson equalised two minutes from time. Sadly, in the replay at Portman Road, Villa won 2–1.

During the 1953–54 first round FA Cup tie against Reading, the Blues conceded a penalty after just 45 seconds. Thankfully, goalkeeper Jack Parry saved the kick and Town went on to win 4–1. The following season, Parry had to leave the field in the match at Swansea after damaging a hand. Wilf Grant went in goal and claimed to have prevented Welsh international winger Terry Medwin from scoring by pulling faces at him.

On 5 November 1966, Frank Brogan scored a hat-trick in a 6–1 win over Northampton Town, two of his goals coming from the penalty spot. This was the first occasion on which the club had scored from two penalties in a Football League match, although the Scotsman was to repeat the feat on a further two occasions. John Wark scored four goals in the 5–1 win over Aris Salonika on 17 September 1980 including a hat-trick of penalties. On 1 March 1980, Town were awarded two penalties in the match against Manchester United and although Kevin Beattie and Frans Thijssen both missed, it did not matter too much as Town ran out winners 6–0.

Ipswich goalkeeper Paul Cooper holds the record from the custodian's point of view, saving an incredible eight of the ten he faced during 1979–80. His technique was to leave a slightly larger gap at one side of the goal, tempting the striker to shoot there.

PERRETT, GEORGE

George Perrett joined Ipswich Town from Fulham in the summer of 1936 and made his debut in the opening game of the following season in a 4–1 home win over Tunbridge Wells Rangers in the club's first Southern League game. The wing-half went on to score four goals in twenty five outings as the Blues won the Championship at the first attempt. Perrett was an important member of the Ipswich side at this time and after the club had been elected to the Football League, he made his Third Division (South) debut in the opening game of the 1938–39 season, a 4–2 win over Southend United.

Unfortunately, his career was interrupted by the Second World War but he returned to the side for the 1945–46 regional league game against Southend United after his demob. It was a game he would probably want to forget as he missed the chance to equalise from the penalty spot in a 2–1 defeat.

When league football resumed in 1946–47, Perrett was a regular in the Ipswich line up and in 1948–49 was an ever-present as the Blues finished seventh in the Third Division (South).

He played the last of his 214 first team games for the club, of which 115 were in the Football League, in a 4–0 home defeat by Notts County on 27 December 1949. Sadly, the popular Londoner died in August 1952, aged only thirty seven.

PHILLIPS, TED

When Ipswich Town won the Third Division (South) Championship in 1953–54, Ted Phillips played in four of the last few games, scoring two goals, one of which came in the 2–1 home win over Northampton Town on the final day of the season as 22,136 welcomed home the champions. The following season he scored both goals on his first appearance in a 4–2 defeat at Hull City and went on to score four goals in twelve games, but in 1955–56 he went to play for Stowmarket in the Eastern Counties League.

However, the club held his registration and in 1956–57 he returned to Portman Road. That season, Town won the Third Division (South) cham-pionship and Ted Phillips broke the goalscoring record with a phenome-nal forty one goals in forty one league games.

He also scored five goals in three FA Cup appearances to become the leading goalscorer in the Football League. Included in his total were five hat-tricks – Colchester United (home 3–1), Queen's Park Rangers (home

4–0), Watford (home 4–1), Shrewsbury Town (home 5–1) and Reading (away 3–1).

In 1957–58, Phillips suffered badly from illness and injuries but still managed to score a goal a game in his eleven appearances including a hat-trick in a 4–2 home win over Bristol City. The following season was not much better, for after having undergone a cartilage operation and then straining his knee ligaments, he only managed to play in half of the club's games. He was back to full fitness in 1959–60 and was an ever-present and top scorer with twenty four goals including hat-tricks against Swansea Town (home 4–1) and Sunderland (home 6–1). The following season the Blues won the Second Division championship and Phillips who was again ever-present, scored thirty goals as he and Ray Crawford terrorised the opposing defences. During this period, he played in 128 consecutive league games.

Phillips and Crawford continued to find the net in 1961–62 as the club won the League Championship at the first time of asking. The Leiston-born forward scored twenty eight goals in forty league games and ended the season with thirty six goals in fifty first team appearances.

He went on to score 179 League and Cup goals for Ipswich before leaving to join Leyton Orient. He scored seventeen goals in thirty six games for the Brisbane Road club before later playing for Luton Town and finally Colchester United where he took his tally of league goals to 199 in 349 appearances for his four clubs.

PITCH

The Portman Road pitch measures 112 yards by 82 yards.

PLAY OFFS

Ipswich Town have been involved in the play offs on three occasions.

The first promotion and relegation play offs were introduced in 1986–87, involving all four divisions. They were used, in part, to reduce the First Division to twenty clubs over two seasons.

In 1986–87, Ipswich finished fifth in Division Two but lost to First Division Charlton Athletic in the play off semi-final stage.

In 1996–97, a Mick Stockwell goal gave Town a 1–1 draw at Sheffield

United but despite scoring two goals inside a minute at Portman Road, the club were held to a 2–2 draw and went out on the away goals rule.

Last season, Town reached the play off stages for a third time, again finishing fifth, and were once more drawn against Charlton Athletic. An own goal by Jamie Clapham gave the Addicks a 1–0 win at Portman Road and though Town battled hard at The Valley they lost again to a single goals with Charlton going on to gain promotion to the Premiership.

POINTS

Under the three points for a win system which was introduced in 1981–82, Ipswich Town's best points tally is the eighty four points in 1991–92 when the club won the Second Division championship. However, the club's best points haul under the old two points for a win system was the sixty four points secured in season's 1953–54, when they won the Third Division (South) championship and 1955–56 when they finished third in the same division. Ipswich's worst record under either system was the meagre twenty five points in 1963–64 when the club finished bottom of the First Division and were relegated.

Ipswich Town produced the widest margin between a club's points total in successive seasons in the same division of the Football League. In the 1961–62 season, they won the championship of Division One with fifty six points but finished bottom the following season with twenty five points.

PORTMAN ROAD

Owned by the Corporation, Portman Road took its name from the ancient office of Portmen in the Borough of Ipswich and was first used by the football team in 1884. The soccer club, which was formed in 1878, chose the name Ipswich AFC, and the rugby club were known as Ipswich FC. In September 1888, the AFC and FC amalgamated under the new title of Ipswich Town and for the next nineteen years played on what is now the training pitch behind the Pioneer Stand. Then it was a cricket pitch, used in summer by the East Suffolk Cricket Club.

Although there was little in the way of ground improvements, Town were one of the first to use goal nets in 1890. Three sides of the ground were bordered by fields and trees and the fourth was overshadowed by the construction, in 1901, of a tobacco processing plant belonging to the Churchman brothers. It was claimed that because the club were tenants, they were not allowed to build stands and instead boards were laid along the touchlines.

However, the club's pride and joy, as it is now, was the playing surface. The cricketers shared that view and to avoid damaging the cricket square it was suggested that Town might prefer their own pitch beyond the cricket boundary. However, it was a number of years before Town began planning their sideways move and although the Corporation did not object, they refused to share the costs.

It was 1905 when the Ipswich Cricket, Football and Athletics Ground Company was formed with a share capital of £2,000 and Town granted a twenty one year lease. There were still no barriers separating the football pitch from the cricket square but there was fencing around the ground and a wooden stand on the Portman Road side, built at a cost of £230.

In 1911, the roof blew off the stand in a gale. Worse damage was caused during the First World War when the army ruined the club's immaculate playing surface. When the hostilities ended, the club tried whippet racing as an extra source of income and new groundsman Walter Wollard kept chickens, goats and sheep in the stand.

With the club still clinging on to its amateur status, Ipswich was the largest town in the country not to have a professional team. It was only in May 1936 when the club's seniority was being threatened by the proposed formation of a team to be called Ipswich United at the Suffolk Greyhound Stadium that the Town committee bowed to public demand.

However, there was still only one stand at Portman Road and all that separated the football pitch and the cricket square was a row of wooden bleachers. During the summer of 1936, iron railings were put up around the playing surface and the first bank of terracing was built up at the North End.

After the club won the Southern League Championship in 1936–37 a terrace similar to the North Stand was built at the Churchmans End, while in the East Stand Ipswich installed 650 seats purchased from Arsenal's recently demolished stand. In 1938, after only two years at professional level, the club was elected to the Football League. Extra terracing was laid and both the East and Churchmans Stands were extended after a gift of £500 from the Supporters Association. Also around this time the ground company went into liquidation and the club became tenants of the Corporation.

The Supporters' Association virtually funded every improvement at the Portman Road ground in the years after the war. In 1952, and at a cost of £3,000, concrete terracing replaced the wooden bleachers. Two years later they found another £3,000 to re-terrace the North Stand. In 1957, the association raised an astonishing £30,500 towards the building of a new West Stand and two years later £15,000 for the Portman Road floodlights.

In 1971 the East Stand was dismantled and a two tier propped cantilever construction called the Portman Stand built in its place. Two years later the Churchmans Stand was re-terraced at a cost of £300,000 and in 1978, after the club had won the FA Cup, executive boxes were added on to the Portman Stand paddock. The terracing in front was converted to seats and around £400,000 spent on safety measures following the introduction of the Safety of Sports Grounds Act.

In 1982, the West Stand was extended. This involved removing the 1957 roof and adding a third tier of 4,800 seats behind, with a new cantilever roof. The project cost £1.4 million but the club recouped part of their outlay by naming the stand Pioneer after their sponsors. In 1990, £105,000 was spent on converting the Pioneer Stand paddock to seating and two years later both ends were also converted at a cost of £550,000 to make Portman Road an all-seater stadium with a capacity of 22,600.

PREMIER LEAGUE

Promoted to the Premier League in 1991–92, Ipswich Town soon established a reputation as the draw specialists, ten of their first sixteen matches ending all square. By mid-February 1993, the club were in fifth place and there was talk of a UEFA Cup place but sadly their form deserted them and they ended the season in a disappointing sixteenth place.

In 1993–94 the club introduced a blanket defence system with either Kiwomya or Marshall as the lone attacker, five at the back and four in midfield. The system worked well on occasions, but it was not popular with the fans although it was this defensive approach that saved their Premiership status. Needing a point to ensure survival, Town drew 0–0 at

Blackburn Rovers. But Ipswich fans were not satisfied with events and at the end of the season first team coach Mick McGivern was moved sideways into a new post as football development officer.

After two years of struggle near the foot of the Premiership, Ipswich finished the 1994–95 season in last place and were relegated to the First Division. During February, March and April, Ipswich went through a period of seven games without a goal, including a 9–0 humiliation at Old Trafford as Manchester United recorded the highest ever Premiership score. The club's total of twenty nine defeats set a new Premiership record as did their tally of twenty seven points – the lowest ever in a season.

PROMOTION

Ipswich Town have been promoted on five occasions. They were first promoted in 1953–54 when they won the Third Division (South) championship, finishing three points ahead of runners-up Brighton and Hove Albion. They were promoted a second time in 1956–57 when the club again won the championship of the Third Division (South) beating Torquay United on goal average after both clubs had ended the season on fifty nine points. Town were promoted for a third time in 1960–61 when they won the Second Division championship, pipping Sheffield United for the title by just one point. The club's fourth promotion in 1967–68 also saw them enter the top flight as Second Division champions.

Town's fifth and final experience of promotion came in 1991–92 when they finished four points ahead of Middlesbrough to win the Second Division title for a third time.

PUTNEY, TREVOR

When he joined Ipswich from Brentwood Town in September 1980, they were one of the best teams in the country and towards the end of that season, they were in line for a unique treble of FA Cup, Football League Cup and UEFA Cup.

Putney made his league debut for the Portman Road club as a substitute for Irvin Gernon in a 1–0 home defeat by Arsenal in October 1982.

During his six years with the Blues, he showed his versatility by wearing nine different numbered outfield shirts and scored nine goals in 127

League and Cup games. In June 1986 he joined Norwich City in exchange for John Deehan and went on to appear in exactly 100 first team games for the Canaries before a £300,000 move took him to Middlesbrough. Sadly, a Gordon Cowans tackle broke his leg and although he made a full recovery, he could not win a place in the Middlesbrough first team. After a spell at Vicarage Road, he joined Leyton Orient before ending his league career with Colchester United.

Q

QUICKEST GOAL

TIMINGS of goals are notoriously unreliable, particularly as you go back to earlier years, and a number of matches have offered a few contenders for the prize. The fastest recorded goal by an Ipswich Town player was scored by Doug Millward after just ten seconds in the 5–0 home win over Newport County on 23 February 1957.

R

RAMSEY, ALF

AS a player, Alf Ramsey was a strong, polished and distinguished defender who joined Portsmouth as an amateur in 1942 and a year later moved to The Dell to play for Southampton. He made his England debut in a 6–0 victory over Switzerland at Highbury in December 1948 before going on to  make twenty eight consecutive appearances for his country. In all he won thirty two caps for England and represented the Football League on five occasions.

In May 1949 he moved to Tottenham Hotspur for £21,000, a record fee for a full-back. Virtually an ever-present in the teams that won the Second Division and Football League titles in 1950 and 1951, he was very accurate with penalties and free kicks and developed into a great reader of the game. In May 1955 after appearing in 250 League and Cup games for the White Hart Lane club, he retired.

He was appointed manager of Ipswich Town in August 1955 and immediately began to refashion the Portman Road side in a manner which was to herald the dawn of a new era. He led the club to the Third Division (South) title in 1956–57, the Second Division Championship in 1960–61 and the First Division Championship in 1961–62.

In January 1963 he was appointed the full-time manager of England. His greatest triumph came in 1966 when England, playing on home territory, won the World Cup for the first and only time. In May 1974 after England had failed to qualify for the finals of that year's World Cup competition, he was sacked. Under Ramsey, England lost only seventeen out of 113 games and had won sixty nine of these. In September 1977 at the age of fifty seven, Sir Alf was appointed manager of Birmingham City. He held office for only six months, before being forced to relinquish the position due to ill health.

RAPID SCORING

On 21 October 1922, Town visited Ealing in a Southern Amateur League game. After taking the lead in the eighth minute, the Portman Road club scored four goals in two minutes to lead 5–0 after ten minutes. Ealing then scored three goals in as many minutes, the final score being 8–5 after Town had led 7–3 at the interval.

When Ipswich beat Floriana of Malta 10–0 at Portman Road on 25 September 1962, they were six goals up at half-time. In probably the most one sided game seen at the ground, Ray Crawford scored five of the club's ten goals, Phillips and Moran netted two each and Elsworthy one.

Town themselves have been on the receiving end of some rapid scoring. In their silver jubilee season of 1960–61, the club won the Second Division championship but they crashed to their heaviest defeat in the FA Cup, losing 7–1 at Southampton. They were six down at half-time, the Saints having scored four goals in seven minutes and George O'Brien scoring a hat-trick in 28 minutes.

RECEIPTS

The club's record receipts are £105,950 for the first leg of the UEFA Cup Final match against AZ67 Alkmaar at Portman Road on 6 May 1981.

REED, BILLY

Rhondda-born winger Billy Reed played his early football with his home club before joining Cardiff City. Unable to make the grade at Ninian Park he signed for Brighton and Hove Albion. He went on to score thirty nine goals in 129 league appearances for the Seagulls before moving to Portman Road in the summer of 1953.

Considered the best right-winger in the division, he possessed exceptional dribbling skill which led to him being dubbed the 'Stanley Matthews of the Third Division'. He made his Ipswich debut in a 2–0 win at Walsall on the opening day of the 1953–54 season, a campaign in which the Blues won the Third Division (South) championship, pipping his former club by three points. In fact, Reed scored in both matches against Brighton, including the winner in a 2–1 win at the Goldstone Ground. Although the club were relegated in 1954–55, Reed was one of Town's best players the following season, scoring twelve goals in thirty league games, including a hat-trick in a 5–2 home win over Walsall. It was during this campaign that he was capped twice by Wales and in the process became the first player to receive full international honours while on Ipswich's books. He won another Third Division (South) championship medal in 1956–57 but played the last of his 171 League and Cup games in which he scored forty six goals, the following season before leaving to end his career with Swansea Town.

REES, DOUG

Doug 'Dai' Rees, already a Welsh amateur international centre-half, joined Ipswich Town from Troedyrhiw in February 1949 with the Blues making a £350 donation to the Welsh club.

He made his league debut in a 1–1 draw at Leyton Orient on 9 April 1949 and went on to play in 385 League and Cup games over the next ten years, including being ever-present in the seasons of 1950–51 and 1955–56. He played in forty one games in 1953–54 and helped the club win the Third Division (South) championship.

When he was appointed club captain the popular defender only scored one goal for Ipswich and that came in a 2–2 draw at Shrewsbury Town towards the end of the 1952–53 season when he was pressed into emergency service at centre-forward.

Rees was selected in the preliminary list of forty Welsh players for the 1958 World Cup but unfortunately did not make the final twenty two. He played his last game for the club at Grimsby Town in April 1959 before hanging up his boots at the end of the season.

RELEGATION

Ipswich Town have only been relegated on three occasions. Their first taste came in 1954–55 when after winning the Third Division (South) championship the previous season, the club finished twenty first in their first season in the Second Division and were relegated. After winning promotion twice, the club were relegated a second time in 1963–64 when they finished bottom of the First Division with just twenty five points, three points adrift of Bolton Wanderers, who were also relegated. Ipswich's third and final experience of relegation came in 1985–86 when they finished twentieth in the First Division and dropped into Division Two along with Birmingham City and West Bromwich Albion.

ROBERTSON, JIMMY

Jimmy Robertson began his footballing career with St Mirren in 1962. Three months after winning his first Under-23 cap against Wales, he moved to Tottenham Hotspur for £25,000. In four seasons at White Hart Lane, he played in 181 League and Cup games. He won a Scottish cap against Wales during the 1964–65 season and scored the first goal for Tottenham in the 1967 FA Cup Final against Chelsea.

In October 1968 he was allowed to join Arsenal in a £55,000 deal which saw David Jenkins travel in the opposite direction.

Robertson never really settled at Highbury and it was no surprise when he joined Ipswich Town for £80,000 in March 1970. He made his debut in a 2–0 home win over Sunderland and scored three goals in the seven games in which he played at the end of that season.

In 1970–71, he missed just two games and he scored five goals in his forty league appearances. When Town travelled to Highbury to play Robertson's former club and champions elect, they found themselves 3–0 down by half-time. Robertson scored two second half goals and was deprived of a hat-trick and equaliser when he netted from a free kick, only for the goal to be disallowed. Having scored twelve goals in ninety eight games for the Portman Road club, Robertson wanted a change and in June 1972 he joined Stoke City for £80,000.

He gave useful service to the Potters before winding down his career with Walsall and Crewe Alexandra.

ROBSON, BOBBY

One of the game's most successful managers, Bobby Robson began his career as an amateur with Middlesbrough but was playing for another local side, Langley Park Juniors when Fulham manager Bill Dodgin pipped Newcastle United for his signature. In May 1950, Robson left his coal-mining job to join Fulham and soon established himself at inside-right alongside Jezzard and Haynes.

However, in March 1956, Vic Buckingham signed him for West Bromwich Albion for £25,000 and in seven years at The Hawthorns he scored sixty one goals in 240 League games. Also during this time, he was converted to wing-half and renewed his partnership with Johnny Haynes when he won the first of twenty full caps for England against France in 1958.

Like Haynes, he lost his international place after the 1962 World Cup but then linked up again with the Fulham maestro when he returned to Craven Cottage for a second spell in August 1962. He played five more First Division seasons, taking his Fulham record to eighty goals in 370 League and Cup games before retiring. After leaving Fulham he moved to North America to manage Vancouver Royals but in January 1968 he returned to Craven Cottage for a third spell, this time as manager.

116

Sadly he lasted less than ten months, being sacked for failing to arrest the club's decline. After a short spell scouting for Chelsea, he was appointed manager of Ipswich Town in January 1969.

The first few years in charge proved tough, but he began to put together a useful side. The club finished fourth in the First Division in both the 1972–73 and 1973–74 seasons. They also finished third in season's 1974–75, 1976–77 and 1979–80 and were runners-up in 1980–81 and 1981–82. The club won the UEFA Cup in 1980–81 but Robson's greatest triumph came in the 1978 FA Cup Final when Ipswich beat Arsenal 1–0.

In July 1982, Robson, who had managed the England B side since 1978, replaced Ron Greenwood as the England manager. Although England failed to qualify for the European Championships in 1984, they qualified for the World Cup finals two years later but lost 2–1 to Argentina in the quarter-finals. After qualifying with ease for the 1988 European Championships, England lost all of their games in the finals. In 1990 he took England to the World Cup semi-finals where they were unfortunate to lose to West Germany on penalties after a 1–1 draw.

In August 1990, Robson had had enough of the limelight as England's manager and took over at PSV Eindhoven. They won the Dutch title in both 1990–91 and 1991–92 but failed to find success in Europe. Robson later mananged Sporting Lisbon before taking charge at Barcelona.

RUNNERS-UP

Ipswich Town have been First Division runners-up on two occasions. They achieved this position for the first time in 1980–81 when they finished four points behind champions Aston Villa. They repeated the feat the following season, again finishing four points adrift of that season's champions, Liverpool.

S

SECOND DIVISION

Ipswich have had four spells in the Second Division. Their first lasted just one season, for after winning promotion from the Third Division (South) in 1953–54, the club finished twenty first and were relegated. After just two seasons back in the Third Division (South) they won promotion again in 1956–57. This time Town spent four seasons in the Second Division before winning the Championship in 1960–61 when they scored exactly 100 goals with Ray Crawford netting forty and Ted Phillips thirty.

After three seasons of top flight football, in 1964–65 the club found themselves in the Second Division for a third spell but after just four seasons they returned to the First Division as champions. During that 1967–68 campaign, they lost just five games in securing fifty nine points. The Blues last spell in the Second Division lasted six seasons culminating in them winning the championship for the third time in their history in 1991–92.

SEDGELEY, STEVE

A Spurs fan as a boy, he trained at the club in his schoolboy days and even appeared in the junior team. However, he was not offered a chance with the White Hart Lane club and joined Coventry City. He made his league debut against Arsenal in August 1986 and soon settled in as a central defender or defensive midfielder. Capped eleven times at Under-21 level by England, he joined Spurs in the summer of 1989 for a fee of £750,000.

Signed to provide defensive stability, he went on to win an FA Cup winners' medal in 1991 and played in 222 first team games before signing for Ipswich for £1 million in June 1994. He made his league debut for the Blues in the East Anglian derby at home to Norwich City on 19 September 1994, a game which the Canaries won 2–1. Over the following seasons he has continued to produce the consistent performances that had been expected of him. He has been troubled by a series of niggling injuries during his Ipswich career, but Sedgeley is a true competitor who plays equally well whether it is in central defence, midfield or as a sweeper.

He made 125 first team appearances for the Blues before joining Wolverhampton Wanderers for £700,000 in the summer of 1997.

SEMI-FINALS

Up to the end of the 1997–98 season, Ipswich Town had been involved in three FA Cup semi-finals, two League Cup semi-finals and a UEFA Cup semi-final, as well as appearances in that stage of the Texaco Cup and Zenith Data Systems Cup.

SIMOD CUP

The Simod Cup replaced the Full Members' Cup for the 1987–88 season. In their first match in the competition, a Clive Woods goal was enough to beat Middlesbrough. In the second round a penalty from Romeo Zondervan took Town through to the last sixteen after Steve Lynex had equalised for West Bromwich Albion following Nigel Gleghorn's opener.

Drawn at home for the third consecutive match, Ipswich faced Watford in the third round and triumphed 5–2 with John Wark scoring two of the goals. Town's other scorers were D'Avray, Deehan and Lowe. In the quarter-finals, Ipswich travelled to Coventry City but went down 2–0.

In 1988–89, two goals from David Lowe helped Town win 3–2 at Oxford United in the first round and earn a second round home tie against neighbours and rivals Norwich City. A crowd of 18,024 saw Simon Milton score the only goal of a close fought game. In the third round, Blackburn Rovers were also beaten by the only goal of the game with Mick Stockwell netting for Town. Reaching the quarter-final stage of the competition again, Town entertained a strong Nottingham Forest team but sadly they again went out, losing 3–1 with Jason Dozzell netting for the Portman Road club.

SINGING THE BLUES

After reaching the play off semi-finals for the second successive season in 1997-98, the club's players turned pop stars with a specially recorded version of the old Ipswich favourite *Singing the Blues*. The club's first team players provided the vocals and the music was by courtesy of the band, The Super Blues. The *Singing the Blues* CD was backed by the club, the *Evening Standard* and Greene King, the club's sponsors. A limited edition of just 1,000 copies were pressed for the bargain price of just £2.99.

SIVELL, LAURIE

Goalkeeper Laurie Sivell played his first game for the club against Liverpool at Anfield in March 1970 when he had to face a penalty at the

Kop End from which Tommy Smith scored the Reds' second goal in a 2–0 win. The following season, Sivell replaced David Best following an injury to the club's first choice Number One and impressed so much that Best was unable to regain his place until the Lowestoft-born 'keeper broke a finger in the home match against Everton.

One of Sivell's best performances in this extended run came in the goal-less draw at Elland Road against the league leaders Leeds United – only the second home point the Yorkshire club had dropped all season.

Sivell's best season was 1974–75 when despite the signing of Paul Cooper from Birmingham City at the end of his loan spell, he made forty league appearances as

Ipswich finished third in Division One. After letting in three goals at Newcastle United on the opening day of the following season, he lost his place to Cooper before winning a recall for the match against Aston Villa.

As the game, which was goal-less, entered its last minute, Sivell made a brilliant save from Chris Nicholl. However, the ball ran loose to Andy Gray and Sivell who dived at the Scottish international's feet to prevent a certain goal, received horrific injuries. He was taken off on a stretcher with blood pouring from a face wound which required eleven stitches in and around his mouth. The brave goalkeeper also lost a number of teeth and suffered a black eye.

He went on to make a full recovery and appeared in 175 first team games before at the end of the 1983–84 season, he gave the game up after suffering for a while with knee injuries.

SOUTH EAST ANGLIAN LEAGUE

Ipswich Town competed in the South East Anglian League for three seasons from 1903–04, winning the Championship at the first time of asking, despite losing their first two matches. In fact, Town won their remaining six matches, including beating Harwich and Parkeston 8–0. In 1904–05, the club finished as runners-up to Colchester Crown and in 1905–06, finished fourth.

SOUTHERN AMATEUR LEAGUE

Ipswich Town were elected to the Southern Amateur League in the summer of 1907 in readiness for the first season of the competition. Their first opponents were Eastbourne, the only other club in the league that was not based in London. Fortunately for the Blues many of the London-based teams opted to make two visits to Suffolk rather than ask Ipswich to visit London. Town beat Eastbourne in their first match 4–1 but ended the season in seventh place.

It was in 1921–22, their ninth season in the Southern Amateur League, that they first won the Championship, losing just once in their twenty matches. That season they had finished one point ahead of Eastbourne but in 1922–23, the roles were reversed. Ipswich were runners-up again in 1928–29 and 1930–31 but sandwiched in between was their second championship success. They finished six points ahead of Eastbourne. Town then won the championship in successive seasons, pipping Catford Wanderers by two points in 1932–33 and Hastings St Leonards by one point in 1933–34. The club's last season in the Southern Amateur League was 1934–35 when they finished fourth.

SOUTHERN LEAGUE

After turning professional, Ipswich Town entered the Southern League for the 1936–37 season and in their first match beat Tunbridge Wells Rangers at home 4–1 in front of a 14,211 crowd. The club won eight and drew four of their first twelve matches, losing for the first time on Boxing Day, 3–1 at the hands of Norwich City Reserves. They secured the title on 17 April 1937 when they beat Yeovil and Petters United 3–0 at Portman Road. Ipswich won nineteen of their thirty matches and only lost three with Jock Carter the top scorer with eighteen goals.

In 1937–38, Town were undefeated in their opening seven matches but after beating Newport County Reserves 8–2, a match in which Gilbert Alsop and Len Astill scored hat-tricks, they lost 5–0 at Barry Town. The club ended the season in third place but in the summer of 1938 they were elected to the Football League.

SPONSORS

The club's sponsors are Greene King. Previous sponsors have included Fisons, Pioneer and Radio Orwell.

STEPHENSON, ROY

Roy Stephenson was playing for Crook Colliery Welfare when he was recommended to Burnley in 1948. After impressing in trials he signed as a professional and although he scored regularly when called upon, he was never quite able to hold down a regular place in Burnley's league side. In September 1956, after scoring twenty eight goals in eighty League and Cup games for the Clarets, he moved to Rotherham United. Little more than a year later he joined Blackburn Rovers, then in the Second Division. He helped the Rovers to promotion to the top flight and also played in every game in Blackburn's run to the semi-final of the FA Cup where they lost

2–1 to Bolton Wanderers. He later had a short spell with Leicester City before joining Ipswich in the summer of 1960.

His fast, direct wing play and pinpoint crosses contributed in no small measure to the century of goals the club scored in the 1960–61 season as they swept to the Second Division championship. During the following season, when the Blues won the League Championship, Stephenson missed only one game and his delivery from out wide on the right continued to serve the prolific Phillips and Crawford.

He scored in Ipswich's Charity Shield clash with Tottenham Hotspur in August 1962 but sadly it was only a consolation in a 5–1 defeat. It was a sign that the bubble was about to burst and after the club struggled in 1962–63, Town were relegated the the following season.

Roy Stephenson played the last of his 163 League and Cup games, in which he scored twenty six goals, in December 1964 and at the end of the season joined Lowestoft Town.

STOCKWELL, MICKY

A one club man who has proved that he can play at right-back, central midfield or on the flanks, Micky Stockwell graduated to the professional ranks during 1982–83 and then waited three years before making his league debut. It came in a 1–0 win at Coventry City on 26 December 1985. Eventually winning a regular place on the left side of midfield in 1987–88, he was injured during a match at Walsall in January 1989 and did not win his place back, this time at right-back, until October of that year. In 1990–91 he played in Town's midfield and missed just two games. An ever-present the following season, he rose to the challenge presented by the new Premier League and ended the 1992–93 campaign as the supporters' 'Player of the Year'.

He was honoured to be handed the captaincy of the Portman Road club at the start of the 1995–96 season but with his game suffering, it was eventually passed on to Tony Mowbray. Still an important member of the Blues' squad, he has played in more than 500 first team games.

SUBSTITUTES

The first Ipswich Town substitute was Dave Harper who came on for Frank Brogan against Charlton Athletic at The Valley on 29 August 1965. The club had to wait until the twenty fifth game of that 1965–66 season for their first goalscoring substitute – Eddie Spearitt – to score in the 2–2 draw with Derby County at the Baseball Ground.

The greatest number of substitutes used in a single season by Ipswich under the single substitute rule was thirty three in 1974–75 but in 1986–87 two substitutes were allowed and in 1989–90 the club used fifty seven. Over the last three seasons, three substitutes have been allowed and in 1996–97, a total of eighty two were used.

The greatest number of substitute appearances for Ipswich has been made by Simon Milton who has come on in sixty four league matches and another eight in cup matches.

Bontcho Guentchev and Simon Milton share the Ipswich record on the matter of substitutes with an extraordinary fifteen league appearances in the substitute's shirt in season's 1993–94 and 1996–97 respectively.

SUFFOLK CHALLENGE CUP

The first Suffolk Challenge Cup took place in 1885–86. Ipswich Town won their way through to the final where they met Woodbridge Asociation. After the first two games were drawn, Town lost 3–1 in the second replay.

In 1886–87, Town won the trophy for the first time, beating Ipswich School in the final 2–1. Despite beating Ipswich Rangers 6–0 in the first round of the 1887–88 competition, Town were knocked out in the next round by Long Melford. The club won the cup again in 1888–89, beating Newmarket 4–0 in the final and scoring twenty two goals in their four matches. The final drew a crowd of just over 3,000, believed to be the largest to have watched a football game in Suffolk up to that time.

SUFFOLK SENIOR CUP

Ipswich Town have won the Suffolk Senior Cup on thirteen occasions. They won the trophy in its first season of 1889–90 when they beat Long Melford in the final 4–1. Their next win was 1895–96 when on their way to the final, they beat Orwell Works 10–0 and Languard Fort 11–1. In the final, Beccles Caxton were defeated 2–0. After beating Beccles College 5–1 in the final of the 1899–1900 competition Ipswich won the cup for five successive seasons from 1903–04, beating Leiston 3–2; Lowestoft

Town 2–0; Haverhill Rovers 6–1; Bury St Edmunds 2–1 and Bury Alexandra 3–0.

The club won it two more times before the First World War, beating Haverhill Rovers 2–1 in 1911–12 and All Saints United 2–1 in 1912–13. After two more successes in 1927–28 and 1928–29 when they beat HMS *Ganges* 2–0 and Woodbridge Town 5–0 respectively, they won the trophy for a last time in 1929–30 when they beat Sudbury Town 6–0.

SUSTAINED SCORING

During the 1956–57 season Ipswich Town won the Third Division (South) championship, scoring 101 goals in the process. Ted Phillips, in spite of missing the first three games of that season, scored forty one goals in forty one games to set a league scoring record for the Blues. He scored five hat-tricks against Colchester United (home 3–1), Queen's Park Rangers (home 4–0), Watford (home 4–1), Shrewsbury Town (home 5–1) and Reading (away 3–1).

T

TALBOT, BRIAN

BRIAN TALBOT began his career as an apprentice with Ipswich Town in July 1968 and before turning professional in August 1972 he had a two year loan spell with Toronto Metros. He made his first team debut for the Portman Road club in a 1–0 win at Burnley in February 1974 and played in the remaining fifteen games of the season, scoring three goals. He spent

seven seasons at Ipswich, playing in 227 first team matches and won five England caps, the first against Northern Ireland in 1977. He was also a member of the Town side that beat Arsenal in the FA Cup Final of 1978.

In January 1979, the all-action midfielder joined Arsenal for £450,000 and at the end of the season was a member of the Gunners' FA Cup winning team against Manchester United and thus became, and still is, the only player ever to play for different cup winning teams in successive seasons.

Talbot created an Arsenal club record in 1979–80 when he appeared in all of the club's seventy first team games and also that season he played

in both losing major finals, in the FA Cup against West Ham United and in the European Cup Winners' Cup against Valencia.

The driving force behind both Ipswich and Arsenal's midfield, his play was built around his great stamina. In just over six seasons at Highbury, he played in a staggering 327 first team games.

Following the signing of Southampton's Steve Williams, he realised his Arsenal days were over and he joined Watford for £150,000 in June

1985. He later played for Stoke City, West Bromwich Albion and Fulham and after serving as chairman of the PFA he went into management with West Bromwich Albion and Aldershot, before moving overseas to take charge of Hibernians in Malta.

TELEVISION

Ipswich Town's first appearance on BBC's *Match of the Day* was on 6 January 1968 when they beat Birmingham City 2–1 with Ron Wigg scoring both goals.

When Ipswich visited The Den to play Millwall in the FA Cup sixth round, the referee had to take both teams off the pitch after a frightening outbreak of crowd misbehaviour. When order was restored, Ipswich went on to win 6–1 with Paul Mariner scoring a hat-trick.

The Portman Road club appeared on the first Sunday that *Match of the Day* was shown, winning 1–0 at Leicester City on 16 August 1980, courtesy of a John Wark goal. However, *Match of the Day* was not the first regular weekly coverage of televised soccer matches. That honour went to Anglia Television's *Match of the Week* which was launched on 23 September 1962 and showed highlights of the Ipswich Town v Wolverhampton Wanderers match of the previous day which the visitors won 3–2.

TEXACO CUP

The predecessor of the Anglo-Scottish Cup, it was launched in 1970–71 and was for English, Irish and Scottish club sides not involved in European competitions. Ipswich only entered in 1972–73 following the withdrawal of two Irish sides because of trouble in that country.

In the first round St Johnstone were beaten 4–2 at home and 2–0 at McDiarmid Park before Wolverhampton Wanderers were beaten by the odd goal in both legs. Facing Newcastle United in the semi-final, a Trevor Whymark goal gave Town a 1–1 draw at St James' Park in the first leg but it took a winner in extra time from Bryan Hamilton to settle the tie in the return leg at Portman Road.

In the final, Ipswich met East Anglian rivals Norwich City and though two goals from Peter Morris gave Town a narrow 2–1 lead in the home leg, the tie was virtually settled after seven minutes of the Carrow Road encounter when Trevor Whymark added to their lead. The Canaries equalised but Norwich-born Clive Woods put the tie out of their reach to clinch the trophy for the Blues. It was an impressive performance by the Portman Road club, which had won seven and drawn one of their eight matches.

THIJSSEN, FRANS

The £200,000 paid to Dutch club Twente Enschede by Bobby Robson in February 1979 for Frans Thijssen was shrewd business by the Ipswich manager. À former team mate of the club's other Dutchman, Arnold Muhren, he guested for Ipswich in Trevor Whymark's testimonial match when Norwich City provided the opposition. He made his league debut in a 1–0 win at Derby County and over the next four seasons was a virtual ever-present, although he missed a few games during the 1981–82 campaign because of groin trouble.

There was talk during his stay at Portman Road that because his contract was soon to expire he may return to his native Holland. But manager Bobby Robson must have persuaded him that there were better times ahead and that he should stay and enjoy them.

Thijssen's time with the club was marked by a high standard of application and skill and his crowning achievement was in 1980–81 when the Football Writers' Association named him as their Footballer of the Year. So Thijssen's name joined the distinguished roll of many of the British game's finest since Stanley Matthews became its first recipient. Thijssen was in fact, only the second foreigner to carry off the accolade, the other being German-born Bert Trautmann, the Manchester City goalkeeper, in 1956.

Thijssen proved beyond doubt that skill in whatever circumstances will always come out on top and turned in a superb performance in his final match at Norwich on 4 April 1983. Promised a free transfer, he joined Vancouver Whitecaps before returning to play league football with Nottingham Forest.

THIRD DIVISION

Ipswich have had two spells in the Third Division (South). After playing their first Football League match at home to Southend United on the opening day of the 1938–39 season, they spent nine seasons in the Third Division (South) before winning the Championship in 1953–54. Prior to that, the club's best position had been fourth in 1947–48.

Relegated after only one season in the Second Division, Town began their second and last spell in the Third Division (South) in 1955–56. That season the club scored 106 goals but finished third. They won the title again the following season with Ted Phillips scoring forty one goals in as many games as Town reached a century of goals for the second successive campaign.

THOMPSON, NEIL

He started his career with Nottingham Forest but on not being offered professional terms by the City Ground club, he joined First Division Hull City early in 1981–82 and made his league debut at Tranmere Rovers in February 1982. After being plagued by injury he was released at the end of the 1982–83 season and joined Scarborough who were then in the Alliance Premier League.

However, in 1986–87 Scarborough won the Championship of the retitled Vauxhall Conference and became the first team to be 'promoted' to the Football League. After missing just five games in 1987–88, he was an ever-present the following season, assisting his team to the promotion play offs.

In June 1989, Ipswich paid £100,000 for the services of this strong-tackling left-back and in his first season at Portman Road he played in all but one game. One of the club's most consistent performers when they won the Second Division Championship in 1991–92, he was ever-present in the first season of the Premier League until he was injured in the FA Cup sixth round tie against Arsenal.

Despite suffering a number of serious injuries, he was a first team regular until the end of the 1995–96 season when after appearing in 246 first team games, he was given a free transfer and joined Barnsley. After loan spells at Oldham Athletic and York City, he joined the Bootham Crescent clubas player/coach.

TOURS

The club's first tour abroad took place at the end of the 1910–11 season when they visited Czechoslovakia. They played two matches against Slavia Prague, losing the first 4–0 and drawing the second 1–1.

TRANSFERS

The club's record transfer fee received is £1.9 million from Tottenham Hotspur for the services of Jason Dozzell in August 1993.

The club's record transfer fee paid is £1.1 million to Bury for Jamiacan-born David Johnson in November 1997.

U

UEFA CUP

IPSWICH TOWN have participated in the UEFA Cup on eight occasions. Their first opponents in the competition were Real Madrid who visited Portman Road on 19 September 1973. Though Town were the better side, they only took a one goal lead with them to the Bernabeu Stadium, that being a Mick Mills shot deflected past the Spanish goalkeeper by one of his defenders. In the second leg, Ipswich held out for a goal-less draw to move into the second round against Lazio.

In a remarkable first leg at Portman Road, Trevor Whymark scored all the goals in a 4–0 win. In the return, Lazio won 4–2 but Town went through to the third round 6–4 on aggregate. The match in Italy had been a violent affair and the culprits Lazio were fined £1,500 and banned from European competition for a year.

In the third round, town faced Dutch side Twente Enschede who had Frans Thijssen in their ranks. A Trevor Whymark goal gave Ipswich a 1–0 win at Portman Road before goals from Morris and Hamilton in the away leg, helped Town to win 3–1 on aggregate. In the quarter-final, the Suffolk club were paired with Lokomotive Leipzig of East Germany and though Kevin Beattie scored the only goal of the home leg, the Germans won the return by the same scoreline after Mick Mills had been sent off. There were no further goals in extra time and the contest went to a penalty shoot out which the home side won.

In 1974–75 Ipswich drew Twente Enschede in the first round and both games ended all square but it was the Dutch side that went through on away goals, having drawn 2–2 at Portman Road.

The following season saw Ipswich draw another Dutch club in Feyenoord, the competition's favourites. However, goals from Whymark and Johnson gave the Blues a 2–1 win in Holland before Woods and Whymark again found the net at Portman Road to give the club a 4–1 aggregate win. In the next round, Town were drawn against Bruges of Belgium and though they won the first leg at Portman Road 3–0, the return in Belgium was nothing short of a nightmare as the home side won 4–0 to take the tie 4–3 on aggregate.

In 1977–78 Town were paired with Landskrona Bois and after a 1–0 win in Sweden Trevor Whymark, the scorer of that goal, hit four in the second leg at Portman Road as Ipswich won 5–0. In the second round, an Eric Gates goal helped the club beat Las Palmas of Spain 1–0 at home before the teams played a great game of open football in the return which ended all-square at 3–3. In the third round, goals from Gates, Whymark and Talbot helped Town humble Barcelona 3–0 at Portman Road but in the return in Spain it was a different story with Johan Cruyff running the game. The Spanish giants won 3–0 and so the match went into extra time but there were no more goals. The game then went to penalties, which Barcelona won 3–1.

Town were drawn against Skeid Oslo in the first round of the 1979–80 UEFA Cup and after a comfortable 3–1 win in Norway, theywon the home leg 7–0 to take the tie 10–1 on aggregate. In the next round, the Blues played Zurich Grasshoppers who were at the time top of the Swiss League. After a goal-less draw in Switzerland, the teams drew 1–1 at Portman Road, to give the Grasshoppers on the away goals rule.

In 1980–81 John Wark scored four of Ipswich's goals in a 5–1 first round first leg win over Aris Salonika of Greece though three of them came from the penalty spot. Town lost the second leg 3–1 but were never really in danger of losing the tie. Wark grabbed two of Ipswich's goals in a 3–0 home win over Bohemians of Czechoslovakia, although once again Town lost the away leg before progressing to the third round where they played Widzew Lodz of Poland. Wark was again on top form and netted a hat-trick in a 5–0 defeat of the Polish club before Town lost 1–0 in Eastern Europe.

In the quarter-final the club enjoyed their first double of the tournament beating St Etienne 4–1 away and 3–1 at home with that man Wark netting in both legs. In the semi-finals a John Wark goal gave Town a 1–0 lead to take to Germany for the return leg with Cologne. Many people thought this would not be enough but a headed goal by Terry Butcher took Town through to the final 2–0 on agggregate. In the first leg of the final, the Blues beat AZ67 Alkmaar 3–0 at Portman Road and although the Dutch side's lead was 4–2 with just 15 minutes remaining, Town held on to win the trophy 5–4 on aggregate, with John Wark scoring a record fourteem goals in the tournament.

As holders Ipswich were seeded for the 1981–82 competition but went out 4–2 on aggregate to one of Scotland's leading sides of the day, Aberdeen, thus ending their defence of the trophy.

Ipswich last participated in the UEFA Cup in 1982–83 but went out at the first hurdle this time to AS Roma. After losing the first leg in Italy 3–0, Town won the return 3–1 with goals from Gates, McCall and Butcher but it was not enough to take them through.

UHREN CUP

Ipswich competed in the Uhren Cup, a pre-season tournament in Grenchen, Switzerland just prior to the start of the 1963–64 campaign. After beating Sparta Rotterdam 4–2, Town beat the host club 5–2 to win the trophy along with a magnificent clock for the boardroom.

UNDEFEATED

The club's best and longest undefeated sequence at Portman Road in the Football League is of thirty three matches between 27 October 1979 and 28 March 1981. Ipswich's longest run of undefeated Football League matches home and away is twenty three between 8 December 1979 and 26 April 1980.

UNUSUAL GOALS

On 26 September 1970 in a Division One match between Chelsea and Ipswich Town at Stamford Bridge, Chelsea's Alan Hudson sent in a shot at an angle which struck the side netting and rebounded into play. As David Best retrieved the ball to take the goal kick, referee Roy Capey signalled a goal and despite protests from Ipswich players and subsequently the club, the result, a 2–1 win for Chelsea, was allowed to stand.

When Ipswich travelled to Turf Moor on 27 March 1971, Burnley's equalising goal in a 2–2 draw was scored by Geoff Nulty, who was credited with the latest Football League goal ever. It was officially timed at one second from the end.

UTILITY PLAYERS

A utility player is one of those particularly gifted footballers who can play in several or even many, different positions. One of Ipswich's earliest utility players was William Cotton. He was equally at home to wing-half or in any of the forward positions. Around the time of the club's entry into the Football League, Jack Edwards showed his versatility by playing in a number of positions.

After the mid 1960s, players were encouraged to become more adaptable and to see their roles as less stereotyped. At the same time, however, much less attention came to be paid to the implication of wearing a certain numbered shirt and accordingly some of the more versatile players came to wear almost all the different numbered shirts at some stage or another, although this did not necessarily indicate a vast variety of positions. In recent years, Mick Mills and Steve McCall have both been talented enough to wear a variety of outfield shirts.

V

VICTORIES IN A SEASON – HIGHEST

IN the 1953–54 season, Ipswich won twenty seven of their forty six league fixtures to win the Third Division (South) championship, the highest in the club's history. In 1960–61 they won twenty six of their forty two Division Two matches to win the title, a feat they equalled in 1981–82 when they finished the season as runners-up in the First Division.

VICTORIES IN A SEASON – LOWEST

Ipswich's poorest performance was in 1994–95 when they won only seven matches out of their forty two league games and finished bottom of the Premier League.

VILJOEN, COLIN

South African-born Colin Viljoen made a remarkable debut for the Portman Road club when he played against Portsmouth on 25 March 1967. After finding themselves two goals down in their first quarter of an hour, Town fought back to win 4–3 with Viljoen scoring a hat-trick. He played in the last ten games of that season scoring six goals, and over the next eight seasons missed very few matches.

In 1967–68 he endeared himself to Ipswich fans when in the local derby against Norwich City, he netted another hat-trick after Town had once again been behind to two early goals and once again won the game 4–3.

In 1974–75 when Town finished third in Division One, Viljoen was voted 'Player of the Year', his form winning him the first of two England caps when he played in a goal-less draw against Northern Ireland at Wembley. Sadly, the following season he suffered from Achilles tendon trouble and was forced to miss most of the season. In fact, he missed the entire 1976–77 campaign after three operations on the tendon.

In the summer of 1978, after he had scored fifty four goals in 372 games he left Portman Road to join Manchester City where he was again hampered by injuries. He appeared in just thirty eight games for the Maine Road club before ending his league career with Chelsea, which he joined in March 1980.

Colin Viljoen

W

WARK, JOHN

AFTER turning professional with Ipswich during the 1974 close season John Wark made his league debut at Portman Road against Leicester City on 29 March 1975, but it was not until 1976–77 that he became a regular in Town's midfield. It was then that he gave early warning of his goalscoring prowess with ten goals in thirty three league appearances. He missed the first half of the following season with injury but returned to help the club to the FA Cup Final where they beat Arsenal 1–0. Ipswich totally outplayed the Gunners and Wark crashed two tremendous shots against the post.

He made his international debut for Scotland against Wales in May

John Wark, centre, fights off England captain Alan Shearer.

1979 and remained a regular selection until 1984. In total he scored seven goals in his twenty nine international appearances.

In three consecutive seasons from 1979 to 1982, the Blues came close to winning the League Championship, without actually clinching it and Wark's goals were instrumental in keeping the club at or near the top. Consolation for these near misses was found in the club's UEFA Cup victory of 1980–81 in which the Scotsman's contribution was outstanding. He scored four goals against Aris Salonika in the first round, a hat-trick against Widzew Lodz in the third round, goals in both legs of the fourth round against St Etienne, a goal in the semi-final against Cologne and goals in each leg of the final against AZ67 Alkmaar which Ipswich won 5–4 on aggregate. In total he scored fourteen goals from midfield in twelve games.

It brought him the accolade of his fellow professionals – the PFA senior award as Player of the Year. The added honour he received, and one which must have been totally unexpected, was that of European Young Footballer of the Year, an award he travelled specially to Italy to collect. He even made an appearance in a film. He had a small part in *Escape to Victory* alongside Pele and Bobby Moore.

In 1982–83 he was top scorer with twenty league goals but had become disaffected and in March 1984 he joined Liverpool for a fee of £450,000 just in time to share in their League Championship triumph. In 1984–85 he was Liverpool's top scorer with eighteen league goals including a hat-trick at West Bromwich Albion. Plagued by injury in 1985–86 he again missed out on a League Championship medal and never won his place at Anfield.

In January 1988 he moved back to Ipswich and proved he had not lost his goalscoring touch with thirteen league goals in 1988–89 and ten in 1989–90. Surprisingly he joined Middlesbrough for the following season but never really settled and in September 1991 returned to Ipswich for a third time as a non-contract player, apparently to help on the coaching side rather than as a first team player.

Remarkably he returned to the team a month after rejoining the club as central defender and held his place to the end of the season as Town won the Second Division championship. In 1992–93 he proved he was still good enough to play at the highest level as the Blues embarked on the first season of Premier League football. In November 1995, in the game at Norwich, he broke the derby appearances record held jointly by Mick Mills and Kevin Keelan when he scored from the penalty spot he broke the goalscoring record as well.

Always an inspiration to those around him, John Wark scored 182 goals in 681 first team games in his three spells at Portman Road.

WARTIME FOOTBALL

In spite of the outbreak of war in 1914, the major football leagues embarked upon their planned programme of matches for the ensuing season but because the War Office commandeered Portman Road, Ipswich Town's season was confined to just a few friendly matches at the start of the 1914–15 season. Also during the hostilities the ground was used both as a training camp and as a storage depot for heavy equipment, with the result that when the war ended, the Ipswich Town ground was in a dreadful condition.

In contrast to what happened in 1914, when war was declared on 3 September 1939, the Football League programme of 1939–40 was immediately suspended. Ipswich had played three league games – against Clapham Orient (away 2–2), Bristol Rovers (home 2–0) and Norwich City (home 1–1) – when the Ipswich Town Board took the decision to suspend football indefinitely. Although the club did not play the Portman Road was used on a number of occasions for wartime matches.

WEMBLEY

On 13 October 1928, before their entry into the Football League nearly ten years later, the Southern Amateur League fixture with Ealing Association was played at Wembley Stadium instead of at nearby Corfton Road where the pitch was declared unplayable. Ipswich won 4–0 in front of a 1,200 crowd with two goals from Rogers and one apiece from Gibbs and Bugg.

WHYMARK, TREVOR

After scoring sixty five goals for the club's Youth and Reserve teams in 1968–69, Diss-born Trevor Whymark was given his first team debut the

Trevor Whymark.

following season in a 1–0 defeat at Manchester City. He appeared in eight games at the end of that 1969–70 campaign, scoring his first goal for the club in a 2–0 home win over Sunderland.

Over the next three seasons, Whymark scored six goals in thirty two league games before establishing himself as a first team regular in 1972–73 when he was joint top scorer with eleven goals. Also that season he netted five goals in the Texaco Cup including one in the second leg of the final against Norwich City. In 1973–74 he again scored eleven league goals but in the UEFA Cup second round first leg match against Lazio, he scored all the club's goals in a 4–0 win. He was joint top scorer in 1974–75 as Town finished third in the First Division before becoming the club's leading scorer for the first time the following season.

Whymark was the club's top scorer again in 1976–77 with more than half his total of thirteen league goals coming in two games. He scored four in the 7–0 demolition of West Bromwich Albion – the first time an Ipswich player had scored four goals in a First Division match – and then a hat-trick in a 5–0 win over Norwich City.

In 1977–78, Whymark scored four goals in a match for the third time as Swedish side Landskrona Bois were beaten 5–0. That performance led to him winning his first full cap for England when he came on as a substitute for Terry McDermott in a 2–0 away win in Luxembourg. Sadly, Whymark damaged his knee ligaments in the Boxing Day match at Norwich and though he played a few games the following season, he was allowed to leave the club and join Vancouver Whitecaps after scoring 104 goals in 335 games.

He later played two games for Derby County before Grimsby Town broke their transfer record to sign him. After scoring sixteen goals in ninety three league games for the Mariners, he ended his league career with spells at Southend United, Peterborough and Colchester United.

WILLIAMS, GERAINT

A hard-tackling competitive midfielder who is always in the thick of things, he began his career with Bristol Rovers and made his league debut for the Eastville club in a 3–3 home draw against Sheffield Wednesday in October 1980. He held his place for the rest of the season despite Rovers' eventual relegation to the Third Division. A regular performer during his

Geraint Williams

five seasons with Rovers, he left Eastville after making 166 League and Cup appearances to join Derby County for a fee of £40,000 in March 1985.

He quickly established himself in a defensive midfield anchor role at the Baseball Ground, assisting the Rams to two consecutive promotion seasons. Williams easily adjusted to the demands of top flight football and was rewarded with the first of thirteen Welsh caps when he played against Czechoslovakia in November 1987. He went on to appear in 321 League and Cup games for Derby but after the Rams missed out in the First Division play offs, he joined Ipswich Town for a fee of £650,000 in the summer of 1992.

On his debut on the opening day of the 1992–93 season he scored Town's goal in a 1–1 home draw with Aston Villa. Though not a prolific scorer from midfield, he has netted a number of memorable goals, perhaps none better than his goal at Reading in 1995–96 when he ran half the length of the Elm Park pitch to score in a 4–1 win for Ipswich. Remaining an important member of the Ipswich side, he has now played in well over 200 games for the Portman Road club.

WILSON, KEVIN

A sprightly striker, Kevin Wilson had trials with Sheffield United and Stoke City before Derby County gave him his chance in league football when they signed him from non-league Banbury United in December 1979. Although he was Derby's leading scorer in 1981–82 his most prolific period was at the start of Arthur Cox's first season in charge when he scored four goals against Hartlepool United in a League Cup tie and a hattrick against Bolton Wanderers before breaking an arm against Plymouth Argyle.

When he recovered, he joined Ipswich Town for £150,000 and made

142

Kevin Wilson

his debut in a 2–1 defeat at Aston Villa in February 1985. Towards the end of that season he scored a hat-trick in a 5–1 home win over Stoke City. With Ipswich he became a Northern Ireland international, winning his first cap against Israel in 1987. Wilson went on to score forty five goals in 116 League and Cup games for Ipswich before the Blues sold him to Chelsea for £335,000 in the summer of 1987.

He continued to score on a regular basis for the Stamford Bridge club and in almost five seasons football, he netted forty seven goals in 172 first team outings before joining Notts County for £225,000 in March 1992. There followed a loan spell at Bradford City before he left Meadow Lane to join Walsall on a free transfer in the summer of 1994.

Capped forty two times by Northern Ireland, this skilful, brave and opportunist striker now plays his football with Northampton Town.

WOODS, CLIVE

Norwich-born Clive Woods had always been a great fan of the Canaries but after they had shown no interest in signing him, he joined Ipswich Town, though he continued to live near Norwich.

He made his debut as a substitute for Ian Collard in a 2–0 home win over Newcastle United on 6 September 1969 and over the next ten years with the club, he baffled the best of defences with his tantalising close skills. When Town won the FA Cup in 1978 by beating Arsenal 1–0, he was voted 'Man of the Match'. He went on to score thirty one goals in 338 games for the Portman Road club before moving to Norwich City in March 1980 for a fee of £70,000, with another £50,000 to be paid when he had made twenty five appearances for the Canaries.

Playing for his home club was an ambition realised for him but after playing in just thirty seven League and Cup games he was given a free transfer by Ken Brown. He had an invitation to play for Twente Enschede of Holland but the terms were not right and he went to play Eastern Counties League football with Newton Flotman.

WORST START

The club's worst start to a season was in 1964–65. It took nine league games to record the first victory of the season, drawing three and losing five of the opening fixtures. The run ended with a 4–2 success over Middlesbrough at Ayresome Park on 26 September 1964 and although the club lost their next match 3–2 at Northampton Town, they were only defeated in a further four games and finished the season in fifth place in the Second Division.

In 1963–64 Ipswich won their opening game at home to Burnley 3–1 but then did not win again for twenty two matches when they beat West Ham United 3–2. The club's next game saw them visit Fulham where they lost 10–1. Not surprisingly, they finished bottom of the First Division with twenty five points and were relegated.

WRIGHT, RICHARD

One of the best young goalkeepers in the country, Richard Wright made his first team debut for his home club on 6 May 1995 in a 2–0 home win over Coventry City. He did not start the 1995–96 campaign as first choice 'keeper but he took his chance with Craig Forrest injured and then away on international duty.

Having come through the international ranks at both schoolboy and youth level, he made the first of his eight appearances at England Under-21 level towards the end of the 1996–97, keeping a clean sheet.

He was an ever-present in 1997–98, a season in which he was asked by Glenn Hoddle to train with the full England team for the friendly international against Chile.

Standing 6ft 2ins and weighing 13 stone, the twenty year old Wright is extremely agile and has now played in 139 first team games for the club.

X

'X'

IN football 'x' traditionally stands for a draw. The club record for the number of draws in a season was in 1990–91 when they managed 18 draws out of 46 matches.

XMAS DAY

There was a time when football matches were regularly played on Christmas Day but in recent years, the game's authorities have dropped the fixture from their calendar.

The last time Ipswich played on Christmas Day was in 1957 when they drew 1–1 against West Ham United at Upton Park. They had played Norwich City Reserves in the Southern League in 1936 and 1937, winning the first meeting 2–0 and losing the second 3–2.

The club's first Football League fixture on Christmas Day saw them beat Queen's Park Rangers 3–1 at Loftus Road. One of the most memorable Christmas Day games was in 1954 when Ipswich visited Anfield and lost 6–2 to Liverpool after being 4–0 down at half-time.

Y

YALLOP, FRANK

HAVING been spotted by Ipswich Town playing in schools football, he made steady progress into the club's professional ranks and eventually, after a wait of over two years, he made his league debut at Everton in March 1984, replacing the injured George Burley. However, it was not until the 1985–86 season that he won a regular place in the Town team at full-back. Unfortunately, it coincided with the club's relegation to the Second Division. He was the club's first choice right-back for the next six seasons and occasionally filled in on the left side or in central defence.

In 1990–91 Yallop was selected for the Canadian national team and went on to win thirty four caps. In 1991–92, when the Blues won the Second Division championship, he lost his place early in the season and played no further part in the successful campaign.

In the first season of Premier League football, he scored two super goals in successive matches but it was a season that was disrupted by World Cup calls. He continued to be an important member of the first team squad and in November 1995 he went on loan to Blackpool.

A few months later, in February 1996 in a bid to cut the Portman Road club's wage bill, the experienced defender was released on a free transfer to join Tampa Bay Rowdies of the new American League after having appeared in 383 first team games in fourteen years with the Town.

YOUNGEST PLAYER

The youngest player to appear in a first class fixture for Ipswich Town is Jason Dozzell who played in the First Division match against Coventry City (home 3–1) on 4 February 1984 when he was sixteen years fifty six days old. He replaced Eric Gates and scored Ipswich's third goal.

YOUNG PLAYER OF THE YEAR

Kevin Beattie won the Professional Footballers' Association Young Player of the Year award for 1974, receiving his award from Don Revie.

YOUTH CUP

Ipswich Town have won the FA Youth Cup on two occasions. The aggregate scores of these two legged finals have been:

1973	Ipswich Town 4	Bristol City 1	(Home 3–0 Away 1–1)
1975	Ipswich Town 5	West Ham Utd 1	(Home 2–0 Away 3–1)

Z

ZENITH

ALTHOUGH Ipswich Town won the FA Cup in 1978 and the UEFA Cup in 1980–81, few fans will argue over which moment has been the finest in the club's history.

After being appointed manager in August 1955, Alf Ramsey immediately began to build an Ipswich Town side which was to win the championship of the Second and First Divisions in consecutive seasons 1960–61 and 1961–62. The club's presence in the European Cup of 1962–63 was one of the game's fairy tales, for just five years earlier, the club members of the Third Division (South).

ZENITH DATA SYSTEMS CUP

The Zenith Data Systems Cup replaced the Simod Cup in the 1989–90 season. Ipswich's first match in the competition saw them beat Watford 4–1 at Portman Road but after beating Wimbledon 3–1 in the third round, they lost 3–2 to Chelsea the eventual winners in the competition's Southern Area semi-finals.

In 1990–91 Town travelled to Plough Lane to play First Division Wimbledon and for the second successive season, the Portman Road club won, this time 2–0. In the next round it took a 90th minute Jason Dozzell goal to defeat Oxford United 2–1 but as in the previous season the club went out of the competition in the Southern Area semi-final, losing 2–0 at Norwich City.

The club last participated in the Zenith Data Systems Cup in 1991–92, winning their first game 3–1 at Bristol Rovers with David Lowe scoring two of the goals. Lowe was on target in the next round but Town were held at home 1–1 by Luton Town before winning 2–1 on penalties. The Portman Road club then travelled to Stamford Bridge to play Chelsea and although Chris Kiwomya scored twice in a 2–2 draw, Town went out 4–3 on penalties.

Romeo Zondervan.

ZONDERVAN, ROMEO

Surinam-born international Romeo Zondervan played his early football with Dutch sides Den Haag and Twente Enschede before joining West Bromwich Albion in March 1982. This most versatile player went on to make eighty four league appearances for the Baggies before being transferred to Ipswich Town for a fee of £70,000 in March 1984.

He played his first game for the club in a goal-less draw at home to Watford after which he was a virtual ever-present in the Town side for eight seasons.

At the end of the 1991–92 campaign in which Ipswich won the Second Division championship, Zondervan, who had rejected several offers to return to Holland to continue his career, left the club after appearing in 274 league games and scoring thirteen goals.

BIBLIOGRAPHY

An Illustrated History of Ipswich Town by Ken Rice. Wensum, 1973.
The Men Who Made the Town. The Official History of Ipswich Town from 1878 by John Eastwood and Tony Moyse. Almeida Books, 1986.
Rothmans Football Year Books.
Ipswich Town programmes.